THE TRANSFORMATION SERIES
Gay Hendricks, *General Editor*

Books in The Transformation Series explore the transitions
of human life and the possibilities for happier, more creative living
through the application of the psychology of adjustment.

Franki Sternberg is a counselor/consultant at the newly formed Creative Counseling Center in San Rafael, California, and is a Ph.D. candidate at the California Institute of Transpersonal Psychology in Menlo Park. Previously she taught in the Cherry Creek Public Schools in Colorado where she created courses on death, dreams, the family, creativity, and communication. She also conducted workshops and seminars for educators. Currently, Franki lives in Tiburon, California.

Barbara Edwards Sternberg, B.A., Sociology, M.A., Urban Sociology, was educated at the London School of Economics, Cornell University, and Denver University. She has taught at Denver University, Colorado Women's College, and the Opportunity School. While active in organizations which are in the process of development or change, and while serving as president of the Denver Woman's Press Club, she has found time to write two books with her husband and to publish nonfiction articles and poetry in a number of Colorado magazines and anthologies.

Exploring Death with Young People

Franki Sternberg
Barbara Sternberg

A SPECTRUM BOOK

PRENTICE-HALL, INC., Englewood Cliffs, N.J. 07632

Library of Congress Cataloging in Publication Data

Sternberg, Franki.
    If I die & when I do.

    (A Spectrum Book) (The Transformation Series)
    Bibliography: p.
    1. Death—Psychological aspects. 2. Death—
Psychological aspects—Study and teaching.
3. Children and death. 4. Youth and death.
I. Sternberg, Barbara, 1923-   joint author.
II. Title.
BF789.D4S74   155.9'37   80-10893
ISBN 0-13-450668-5
ISBN 0-13-450650-2 pbk.

Editorial production/supervision
and interior design by *Heath Lynn Silberfeld*
Manufacturing buyer: *Cathie Lenard*
Cover design by *Lana Giganti*

Prentice-Hall International, Inc., *London*
Prentice-Hall of Australia Pty. Limited, *Sydney*
Prentice-Hall of Canada, Ltd., *Toronto*
Prentice-Hall of India Private Limited, *New Delhi*
Prentice-Hall of Japan, Inc., *Tokyo*
Prentice-Hall of Southeast Asia Pte. Ltd., *Singapore*
Whitehall Books Limited, *Wellington, New Zealand*

Contents

Foreword

I am deeply moved by this book. *If I Die and When I Do* speaks to something so deep in us that it cannot help but bring up strong emotion in any sensitive reader. For anyone who works with young people, it is an especially valuable gift.

I remember well the evening I first sat down with the book. Before I had finished thirty pages I was vividly reliving some of the death experiences that had shaped my life. I cried long-forgotten tears about the deaths of my grandparents, two of my favorite aunts, several friends, and a pet that had died when I was thirteen. I cried also for some of the people who speak through the book and for the little deaths that each of us experiences each day in life. After I finished the book I went outside to take a walk. The stars seemed to glimmer with a brighter intensity, and life seemed especially sweet.

I have known Franki Sternberg for a number of years. She is a beautiful person and a gifted teacher. As you will soon see, Franki, assisted by her mother and father, also has a facility for capturing the spirit of young people as they explore death and life. Although the main subject of the book has to do with death, *If I Die and When I Do* is really about life. After reading it, we know more about how to live our lives with care, kindness, and verve.

Children are the essence of life. There is part of them that is forever trembling on the brink of the next discovery. To a kid, things are always about to look up, even when they are looking grim. As children grow up, though, the "real" world begins to corrode their natural vigor and audacity, and our kids begin the long, slow death of the spirit that can only be transcended in adult life with persistence and work on oneself.

I hold Franki in high esteem. She is deeply committed to her own evolution and to furthering the evolution of those with whom she comes into contact. Her mother and father, at whose warm Colorado home I have spent many happy times, are people any of us would treasure as parents. Reading the book, though, you too may come to feel that the authors, regardless of how gifted, were really channels through whom the children themselves could find voice. And so I feel the book is by children, for the child in all of us, to nurture that part of us which is forever seeking greater meaning in death and life.

GAY HENDRICKS
COLORADO SPRINGS, COLORADO

Preface

In order to respect the privacy of the students whose thoughts and experiences appear throughout this book, we have not used their names. We want particularly to thank and honor all the parents who so kindly allowed us to print their children's words, and the children themselves, because they enriched the book and our lives beyond measure.

We would like to say something about how this book came to be. I, Franki Sternberg, taught the classes from which the book emerged. When the first person is used in the book, I am speaking. My mother, Barbara Sternberg, sensed the power of what was happening in the classes and encouraged me to save materials and keep notes. Barbara also suggested that the material become a book, and she did the original organization and first draft. From the beginning we wanted the project to be as joyful and full of growth as the classes had been. We agreed to work together only when the process felt effortless. We also agreed to honor and acknowledge each other's rhythm of work. Thus, the writing of the book was a process of growth and liberation for both of us, and for our relationship. When the book was finished, we had a stronger bond as mother and daughter, and as adults.

I would like to acknowledge some of my own teachers, friends, and colleagues who were and are important in my life and in my growth as a teacher. I am deeply grateful to Shirley Ward, Billie Straub, Patrick Sternberg, John Sternberg, Jennifer Sternberg, Eugene Sternberg, Lynn Schukar, Elizabeth Schneider, Cathy Schmidt, Ralph W. Remmes, Walter Parker, Miles Olsen, Tom Olkowski, Gabrielle H. Olejniczak, Ann Morrow, Cleo Landon, Carl Koonsman, Tony Kaempfer, Darrold Isaacson, Gay Hendricks, Donna Gullickson, Muriel Edwards, Claudia Czajkowski, Jack Cousins, Dee Coulter, and Buddy Blom.

We dedicate this book to the hundreds of young people who participated in the classes on death.

Transformation Via a Course on Death

Death Is a Sudden Push
into a Silent World

If I die and when I do
I'll be gone, but not for long.
I'll be back to hear the song
of sweet wisdom.

This poem, like all the poetry, stories, and illustrations in this book, was created in a middle-school class on death and dying. The writers and artists were 11-, 12-, and 13-year-old young people.

I hadn't planned to teach a course about death. For a social studies class demonstrating how to deal creatively with controversy, I selected six touchy issues for discussion. When we began talking about death, though, something in the classroom atmosphere changed. There was a still attentiveness. I discovered that this subject touched a chord that vibrated deep inside my students and me.

This was the first time that many of the kids had talked freely about the taboo topic of dying. Most had never shared their private experiences with others.

As one student wrote,

People relate to things
by a word,
but Death is one
seldom heard.

It is not easy, as an adult, to see beyond the myth of the happy childhood. It took me a while to acknowledge fully that all students by the age of 11 had personally encountered death. A curiosity bordering on fascination was already present; the involvement had begun.

I went on to develop a nine-week course on death and dying. I taught it for three years and it transformed my teaching and my life. In the classes we all shared our first experiences with death. We discussed the ways different cultures say farewell to the dead, and we had a mortician speak to us about the American way. We listened in deep silence as both a mother and a young male teacher described how they were coming to terms with their own terminal cancer. A team told us about their work in suicide prevention.

In a discussion about ideas on life after death, some students became fascinated with reincarnation. I invited a speaker who was a psychic and totally committed to a belief in rebirth. We had spirited debates about such issues as euthanasia, the use of medicine and technology to keep people alive, and the difference between living and continuing to exist. Through guided imagery experiences, students imagined their own deaths and their funerals, if they chose to have them. They visited graveyards and funeral homes and, in general, explored the world of death.

The ground rules for our class sessions were set originally by the principles of fair, honest, and supportive discussion. I tried to respond to the young people's zest for

IF I DIE & WHEN I DO

information and experience, allowing the discussion to flow from death to the content of dreams and fantasies and the possibility of valid experiences outside the realm of the five senses. We learned how to respect our own views, to acknowledge that they could change, and to honor the opinions and beliefs of others even if they were radically different from our own.

Far from being morbid, the classes were alive and filled with vitality. One day we were watching a sensitively produced filmstrip about the story of Eric, a boy who had died of leukemia. A mother came in to visit her daughter's class. It was pretty far along in the nine-week course, and the kids were sitting comfortably, as was I, stopping the strip from time to time to discuss what was going on in the lives of Eric and his mother. Stepping back. Getting some distance and perspective. Death was becoming less awesome, less unthinkable, more approachable for the kids. The mother had to leave. Her daughter came to class the next day and told me that her mother could only think with horror of her own children dying. Furthermore, she felt it inappropriate to deal with the subject at all. I thought that the mother could have learned a great deal from her daughter, who was able to look at death and didn't experience it as morbid.

Within these classes about death, a loving atmosphere evolved. I felt privileged to participate in the complex and wonderful internal worlds of these young people. We shared pain with one another, as well as grief and loss. In one class, we cheered on a boy who was winning a tough battle with a menacing Fat Lady in his dreams and fantasies. We all felt a part of his victory. Often we sat in silence, deeply moved by a poem or story that captured the anguish of losing a friend or the sheer joy of still being alive. A talented young woman read us her short story about a young girl whose brother had been killed. In the story, the sister moved through guilt, rage, and denial into acceptance of the death and renewed life for herself. When the story ended, the entire class broke into spontaneous applause.

Tuning in to the students enabled me to touch the deeper parts of myself, and in so doing I deepened my relationship with the child inside me. The lines of distinction between teacher and students faded as we recognized how much each of us had to learn and to teach. Until I had begun this class, I had not seen so clearly how singular and powerful young people can be. It became part of my purpose as a teacher to enable children to remember who they were and to encourage them to live out their full potential.

Shortly after I left this teaching position, I reflected on what had happened to me as a result of dealing openly with death in the company of hundreds of young people.

I wrote,

TO THE CHILDREN IN ALL OF US

who, at times, cry out
and, at times, gently touch
as if kindly to remind
the other parts of us
of their existence.
They ask acknowledgment and expression.
There is much to learn from
those child parts of ourselves.
There is much to gain
from loving and encouraging
our "little people"
and hearing
their large, cleansing
voices.

It is, as some suggest,
a most difficult task
to allow for the existence of,
to regain connection with,
to encourage the growth of,
our child selves.
I had said goodbye
to many parts of myself—
youthful, active, curious,
physical, sensual, intuitive,
exploring, opening selves—
when I began teaching in a public school
in my twenty-fourth year.

My students were from eleven
to fourteen years old.
I found that through a process
of teaching them for four years—
of being with these people—
I began to reconnect with more of me.

Children are closer than most of us
to their child selves,
but at this particular age
there is transformation
taking place. Decisions
are being made about
just which parts must go.

I watched many children die
as these young people became older.
To many of them, this was a conscious,
difficult, sad decision.
Their view of older
was so limiting, due in large part
to the limited people
who taught them
the meaning of adult.

To watch a child jump into the abyss
while other, far less flexible, selves
were activated and applauded
was for me a death-rebirth process
taking place daily in my classroom.
I viewed it mostly as death.

For me to affect in any way
the students' views of choices open to them,
my child selves had to be reborn,
granting these young people space
to choose to keep the children in themselves.

It was as I experienced
the wisdom of the children
that my teaching was no longer
a job to be endured,
robbing me of time
to enjoy my life.

We began to touch each others' lives,
As I was touched,
my ability to touch
increased a thousandfold.

We all wanted more
than was already there.
I shared in their despair,
I shared in their rejoicing.

When you are a child,
your child with other children,
you find the boundaries changing
of what it means to be alive.

Sharing Experiences about Death

All I Can Remember
Is Feeling Left Out of Something Important
that I Was Supposed to Cry About

Frequently I started the course off by sharing my own experiences with death. The tables were arranged in a circle so that everyone could see everyone else. I was in the center. I told the stories with feeling and in detail because it was important to me that students saw me as vulnerable and fully human. Sometimes I took a guitar and ended with a song that a 19-year-old friend, who had died in an automobile accident, had taught me. Almost always there were tears.

This was the beginning: a statement that the class was a permission-giving space for fears, silence, sorrow, joy. A place where people could allow one another to cry. It seemed important to the opening-up process that I be the first to risk sharing my story. I recognized these middle-school students as resilient human beings who could grow as a result of feeling the full range of emotions.

Some of my own questions about death came from a gnawing dissatisfaction with the way my grandmother had died a year or so before. To many of the students, grandparents were shadowy figures who lived in distant cities and were dutifully visited once a year. But my grandmother was an integral part of my large family while I was growing up. I loved her, hated her, took pride in her, resented her; in short, I was involved with her in an ongoing human relationship.

Until she became ill with cancer, she had been a remarkable fountain of energy and activity. Her joy in life was doing for others. She had a demanding job in psychiatric nursing and participated fully in the program of a busy church. And yet she had time to bring us all sorts of bottles, gadgets, and operating gowns from the hospital, to fix little crust-free sandwiches when we played airplane, and to sew Hallowe'en costumes for us.

She was 69 when they operated on her. The surgeons told us that cancer had spread throughout her abdomen. Chemotherapy was at best a delaying action. Her remaining life span was probably six months, three years at the very most.

Three years later, looking back on the time from the surgery until her death, my mother and I felt that much of the process of her dying had been handled badly—by us as a family, by her doctors, by the institutions with which she was in touch—especially the hospital and her church— and by herself. We were all kind, considerate. We spent time with her, and we made sure she was comfortable. But we were not able to talk with her about the most important event that was happening to *all* of us, which was her dying.

Of course, like the good sport she was, she played the game. During the last month in the hospital she was full of painkilling drugs, swollen with the poisons accumulating in her body. She looked into my eyes one day and asked, "When am I going home?" I felt grief about the barriers to openness that we had all created. My gut said to speak with her honestly: "I don't think you're going to leave the hospital this time, Granny." My head and my voice said, "Soon." I learned in that moment what seminars on dying now tell us: the dying need to participate in their own death process. They need to share their fears, hopes, and anger. They need to work through the stages of their own grief and loss, so finally they can come to terms with their departure from this life.

After sharing my experiences about my grandmother's death with the students, I asked them to write a paper discussing their first significant encounter with death. They were to include as many details as possible about their own feelings at the time, how the death was—or was not—handled by various members of the family, the funeral—if there had been one—and what death meant to them at the time of the experience. I asked them to write about any smells, sights, or sounds that they could recall.

As the papers arrived, a joyful and surprising process began. At the beginning, many students were nervous about having their papers read aloud, so I read them anonymously. Inevitably, the stories were so touching and so real that in a short time individual students wanted the

class to know which experience was theirs. Eventually, because of the supportive air in the classroom, the students were reading their own work and that of others aloud.

We would sit in a circle on the floor and listen to these moving tales for hours.

In retelling their first significant experiences of death, some children wrote about a pet, others wrote about a grandparent, a sibling, a parent, or a close friend. Often the death had been ignored, denied, or suppressed. Sometimes the emotion had been displaced onto some other object or event. If the children were lucky, they could recall a sharing of the grief and a time of genuine mourning.

The stories indicated that the children learned much from the way death was handled by others. Sometimes the messages they received were honest, heartfelt, and helpful.

We went away to spend Christmas with relatives. Our dog ran out of our cousins' yard. We searched and searched for him, but then we had to leave. We put ads in the papers and on radio programs. New Year's Eve my aunt called and said a lady had told her they had found our dog frozen to death. We were having a New Year's Eve party, and just before the guests came, our whole family cried for a long time, even my Dad. That's when I had the warm feeling.

My grandfather, who is 72 years old, and my grandmother, who is 68, have written up their wills, decided on headstones, and where they both want to be buried. My grandfather is a small-built man who stands close to 5' 10". Because of major operations years ago, when they removed most of his stomach, and calcification of his lungs, he only weighs 85 lbs. He sleeps so still his electric watch stops. Every morning when he wakes up, he has to try to get oxygen; he has a hard time breathing. He has to take things very slow, can't eat much, has to take a nap every day, can't talk long and suffers all the time because of his struggle to breathe.

Finally, Granddaddy, Grandma and our family have realized that his time left won't be much longer. When my own father was ill early this year, Granddaddy wrote him a beautiful letter about how Dad shouldn't scare the breath out of a man who can't breathe anyway. Another time he wrote to thank my Dad for a Christmas present. He said that he and Grandma usually wait till Christmas to open gifts, but now he only lives for today because he doesn't know how many tomorrows he will have.

We called my grandparents the other night. Granddaddy told my father he would love to get a puppy. We all put 2 and 2 together and figured he wants a dog so when he goes he won't leave my grandmother alone by herself. He has accepted death and his conclusion, where a few years ago he feared it. We all know he will leave us soon, but we have beautiful memories.

Often, though, the messages children received at the time of a death were confusing.

The first time I ever had to deal with death in a person was when my grandfather died. I was at school, and when I got home my mother told me that he had died the night before. I asked her why she didn't tell me in the morning. She said she didn't want to ruin my Hallowe'en day at school and the party afterwards. I cried for a long time after that.

We cried together when one young woman, age 13, told us that her mother had died a year before. Because of archaic hospital rules preventing children under 14 from seeing dying people, this girl had been unable to say good-bye, or to conclude in any way, her personal involvement with her mother. A year later, the pained and helpless expressions on her face made it clear that this unfinished business would be with her for a long time.

Naturally, one of the common first experiences with death for junior high students is that of a grandparent or great-grandparent.

My Grandpa died of a diabetic disease. He was my favorite Grandfather. We would always go hunting or fishing together. My Dad would always be too busy working. Me and my Grandfather were doing something together until the day he died. I thought the world would end. Then I tried not to think about it. But once in a while I get memories of his death.

I walked in the house and my little sister said my Mom wanted to talk to me. I saw her crying in the family room. My heart just stopped. She said, "Grandpa died this afternoon." I just stood there. When it finally registered, I went screaming "NO! NO! NO!" up the stairs. The next day we went to my Grandma's. I had been in shock all the time. I cried at the mention of his name. I'm over it now, but I always remember what a sweet man he was.

When my grandfather died it was hard to believe at first. After I realized he was really dead, all I felt was empty, like

IF I DIE & WHEN I DO

a big chunk of me went right along with him. Now, I won't even go to see where he is buried because I want to remember him the way he was.

When my grandfather died I was heartbroken because we went horseback riding almost every week and he gave me and my brother things. When he died I knew I would never see him again.

A year ago last summer my grandpa got very sick, so my Mom decided to go to Illinois to see him and take my brother and me with her.

I was prepared for him to die because we knew he had leukemia. But I had a very empty feeling when he went because I had been with him and talked with him only 2½ weeks before. It was like I was all alone. I cannot remember if I cried or not, but I remember that terrible lonely and empty feeling. Sometimes I want to go to Illinois and I actually expect him to be there.

I was 4 when my mother received a long distance phone call from her home in Luxembourg. Three days later we were there. I saw my Grandfather lying in bed. My mother said he had cancer of the lungs. I always stayed by his side. One morning I saw my Grandmother and my Mom crying. I ran into his room and saw him with a sheet over his head. Two days later I went to his funeral. And now, I miss him very much and I wish he was still here.

GRAM

I looked at her
And she was dead.
I touched her hand
It was cold, like lead.

Her face was white
And very old.
But she looked kind
And dear as gold.

There she lay
In a dress of white.
Her body seemed fragile,
I cried at the sight.

She used to tell stories
About my Dad.
Never again!
I was sad.

I came home from school and my Dad was the only one home. We went to my Grandma's house for dinner and all her mirrors were covered. I asked my Dad why. He said that it is a tradition that you did, if someone real close to you died. Then I asked, "Where's Grandpa?" My Dad said he had died. I took it pretty hard. I remember my Grandpa because I had to say something about him in my speech for my Bar Mitzvah.

When my grandfather died I was so scared, mostly for my grandmother because I knew it was really a lonely experi-

ence. Ever since then, I've been afraid that everyone I love will die.

"Papa," my grandfather, died two weeks before Christmas. It was a very sad Christmas. I was closer to him than anyone else in my family, except my Dad. We went to his funeral and me and my brother cried and cried. He had always wanted a Polaroid camera, and that Christmas he was getting one, too!

For many children grandparents lived far away and were seen only rarely. When death came, the kids were expected to feel sadness, but in fact the death was not very meaningful to them.

It was my Grandma who died. There were lots of flowers and it seemed sort of dark in the room. I felt very funny. A lot of people were crying. I smelt nothing and I felt nothing.

I came down the stairs to eat breakfast and my mother told me my great-grandmother had died. I tried to cry but I couldn't. I tried to feel really bad, but I couldn't. The death just didn't register and it still doesn't. When my grandfather died this summer I couldn't cry or feel bad. Death does not faze me.

I have only experienced death once and that was three years ago when my grandmother died. I remember one

*day coming home, my sister called me into another room
and told me that my grandmother had died. All I could
hear was a lot of crying and a car going by.*

**Some young children are exposed, without prepara-
tion, to the experience of seeing bodies in open caskets.
Many students in the classes said that they would choose
not to see the body since their primary concern was remembering the person alive. Others acknowledged that it
helped them to be realistic about the death. All agreed that
they would want the choice to be theirs.**

*During the rosary session the casket was open. They had
put make-up on my grandmother, so you would think
she was still alive.*

Child, about 8 at the time

*I had never seen a dead person before and didn't want to
go up and see him. When I finally went, I remember
thinking it looked as if he were sleeping. All I wanted to
do was to touch him, so I put my hand on his hand. I
drew it back quickly because of the way it felt. It was cold
and unreal.*

Death of Grandpa—child about 10

*At my uncle's funeral, they started a line to view the
body. I didn't know what to do, so I got up and joined the
line. My Mom pulled me back quickly and said that I
didn't want to see. But I said I did, so she looked at my
Dad and then said, "Alright." When I saw my uncle, I*

couldn't believe it. He looked very pale and his face was a light blue in some places. I had dreams about this for a couple of weeks.

Child about 7—had never met the uncle

For both children and adults, the hardest deaths to accept and understand are those of the young.

SEEMS IT ONLY HAPPENED YESTERDAY

He was only six months old, vivid and unafraid of any-
*   thing,*
If he was still alive, if he could have lived,
My father's attitude wouldn't have changed
and my mother wouldn't cry all day long
December twenty-one.

And I wouldn't dream over and over
of the many times I've cried,
Remembering how my little brother died,
And I wouldn't scream while in a dream
It wouldn't haunt me, no,
Seems like it only happened yesterday.

If I could only bring him back
to see what he would look like,
Oh! if I only could,
Then I wouldn't have to remember or dream,
I could just think of tomorrow and yesterday.

If only that stupid piece of string had not
Cut short his life, he was much too young,
But while he was sleeping
It wrapped around his neck and he died.

Then I wouldn't dream over and over
Of the many times I've cried
Remembering how my little brother died,
And I wouldn't scream while in a dream
It wouldn't haunt me, no,
Seems like it only happened yesterday.

One boy had always impressed me as a sensitive person. He was considered by many of the staff as a troublemaker and was categorized as a student who needed 'special help.'

One of the few papers he turned in to me described how he was coming home from school one day with his twin brother, and they had stopped off at a friend's house. He put his books down so he could play. After a short while they went home, where they found their parents getting ready to go out to dinner. He got into the shower, then remembered that he had left his books at the friend's house. Since he couldn't go right then to get them back, his brother went for him. His parents left, but in just a few minutes, they were back. His mother was screaming that she had seen his brother hit by a car. His parents left for the hospital, and when they came back an hour later his Dad told him his brother was dead.

When we talked about this death in his life, I felt sad about the weight of the burden he had shouldered alone. He told me the event was never discussed in his family, and it was clear that the guilt about his brother's death had made a deep mark on his life.

Other children wrote of the deaths of people close to them.

My uncle was 26 when they found he had something
wrong with his kidneys. The only way for him to stay alive

a little longer was to stay on a kidney machine three days a week, for 8 hours each time. He had five children to bring up, and when he was not on the machine he was working so he could bring some money home. Fourteen months later he died. I still miss him and I think my aunt never got over it.

About three weeks ago there was a death in our family that really affected me more than any other death I have experienced. One of my cousins died. He was only 18. The news came to us by telephone. I almost went into shock. My mind just formed a total blank. Then it hit me. HE'S DEAD AND I'LL NEVER SEE HIM AGAIN. I just couldn't stand it, it didn't make any sense at all. He was young, strong, and smart. Why him?

Some really good friends of my parents came to have dinner with us. They brought their only son, who was about 21. My brother and I got to be friends with the guy. After about two months, my Mom got a letter from the boy's mother. It said that the boy had died. He had diabetes and forgot to take his insulin. He went into a coma.

About four months after, the father died. His wife told my parents he must have died of a broken heart because nothing else was wrong with him.

It was a sad experience for our family. We didn't say much to each other, just sat around thinking. Even though the weather was hot and sunny, it felt cold and dark.

My first experience of death was the wife of a friend of my father's. She was in her early twenties, and had cancer. They operated and as a result she could not have children. I felt sorry for her because she was such a beautiful woman. They thought they got all the cancer, but they didn't. Five years later, she died. She had a beautiful death. She was sitting in her husband's arms in their family room. She rested her head on him, and he thought she was sleeping, but she was dead.

When my Mom told me of her death I started to cry. But when she told me how painless and peaceful it was, I was happy that she was rid of the pain and misery life gave her.

There was my friend's little sister. She got cancer and she had to take a lot of medicines, but it was too late to do anything about it and she was going to die anyway. She didn't quite know what was the matter with her, she was only 6 or 7. Her hair fell out and she had to wear wigs. She died about 4 months ago. I really was upset because she used to follow me around everywhere when I was over at their house.

My friend invited me to go on a boating trip with him at the reservoir. My stomach wasn't feeling good, so I decided to sit on the side and watch. My friend's Dad put the boat with the wave instead of against it and the boat turned over. His Dad took off his lifejacket and went looking for his little sister. But his little sister was under the seat. His Dad went down and got caught in the weeds and died, and so did his sister.

DANNY

Lately I've been thinking
Of how it was back then.
You were eleven and I was ten.

All the games we used to play
When the sun would shine
And you were mine all day.

We were so old but yet so young
We used to act all grown-up—
You were twenty and I nineteen.

We acted dumb, I'll admit,
But I remember we were a hit.
Our parents used to laugh a lot.

When you died part of me died too,
I always wished I could marry you.

Then there were the young people whose parents had died.

My father died in a truck that went off a bridge. I was about 4 or 5. I can remember him, but not very good. He was nice as I can remember. Then my Mom got a job and was a widow for a few years with five kids. Then she got married. My father right now is very nice. And they had a baby.

It all started when my Mom had been in the hospital for three to five months. And I only got to see my Mom about once a month. One night my aunt told me to pray for my Mom, and I was praying that whole night. The next morning everybody was just sitting around. And my aunt was sitting in the rocking chair in the corner. So I asked everybody what was the matter and they told me right out that my Mom had died this morning. I didn't believe them at first, but then they all looked seriously, so I believed them. So I went out and our paperboy asked if my Mom was okay and I said, "Yes," and went up and played basketball. And I couldn't even play basketball because my mind was too much on my mother's death.

When my father died I was only six and I didn't understand much. My Dad had a funeral and my Mom cried and I think that's the only reason I cried. I didn't realize I would never see him again, until I was older in second grade and there in school I was crying. The teacher thought I was sick and she asked me what was the matter. I said, "My Daddy's dead."

There were deaths taking place in some people's lives while the course was going on. To watch a young woman trying to come to terms with the death of her father was a deeply touching experience.

There is a speaker here now talking about her cancer. There are so many things I would like to ask her. But, the more I ask, the closer I feel to tears. I want to know how my father felt, but I can't really think she knows, because she is still alive. I wish I could just leave, but I feel trapped. I can feel myself losing control. I wish the bell would ring. The more she talks the more I remember about Daddy.

*I've got this awful tightening in my stomach. It is very
frightening to know that it happened seven months ago
and it still shakes me up so much. I think it will always
haunt and scare me. The bell's about to ring. Thank God!*

**It is the death of a pet, for most kids, that first breaks
their hearts and shatters the illusion that life is forever.
Pets are often dear and beloved friends of children. From
my experience with my students I learned how important it
is to allow and encourage children to freely express the
range of their feelings about the death of an animal friend.**

*Did you ever have
a pet die?
You'd cry and cry.
It made me want to die,
but instead I would cry,
"Why do we die?"
Why?*
   Why?
     Why?

*My first death experience was when my grandfather died.
I was only 7, so I didn't really care that much. But when
my cat died, I felt like the end of the world was coming.*

*My first experience with death was when my pet mouse
died. I loved him very much, he was one of my best
friends. I remember how he use to crawl up my sleeve
and make a nest in my hair.*

My dog was put to sleep when I was eight and just starting to understand what death meant. When I came home from school and my mother told me he was gone and was never coming back, I fell apart. For a whole week I would cry all night and remember what he looked like. I can still remember the smell on my fingers after petting him.

I was only four years old when my pet frog died. I went down in our basement and found him dead on the floor. I screamed. My father took him outside and we buried him. I remember the sound of the shovel. My Mom had her arm on my shoulder and I was crying.

I had always wanted a gerbil or two. I had watched them in the pet stores and they were so cute and frisky. Two days before Thanksgiving my grandmother got me two baby gerbils. On Thanksgiving I got them out and played with them and let them run on my stomach. After a while, only one was still on my stomach. Very carefully I got up, watching where I stepped, to look for the other one. I looked back where I had been lying and there was the other one squished to death. I let out a big scream and I ran to get my Dad, who cleaned him up. I cried and cried. My grandmother got me another gerbil, but to this day I can still see that poor little gerbil squished to death.

The first experience I had with death was when my guinea pig died. Her name was Petunia and they told me she would live for two and a half years. I had wanted a *pet for a long time and I was very happy. One day I went to get her, because I felt like I had been ignoring her, and she was dead. I was heartbroken. She had helped me when I was lonely. But I knew she had lived a good life of seven years. Whenever I have a problem, I go to my pets. Now I have a cat, dog, and two horses, so I always have someone to talk to. But none will ever be the same as Petunia.*

I was 8.
I got my own pet.
A rat.
Everyone thinks rats are dirty sick ugly creatures.
Not Sam.
She was white with a black head and a black stripe down her back.
She trusted me so much.
Her life was short.
I always let her run around my room.
When I called her, she came.
One day I came home. She was in her cage motionless.
I picked her up. She moved funny.
I quickly put her in a shoebox with some Kleenex.
My Mom was not home.
Sam climbed weakly out and into my hands.
I knew she would die.
I put her in the shoebox on my bed.
I watched her die.
Goodbye, Sam.
You'll never be here again.
I dealt with this alone.
It helped me.
She was a good rat.

I remember my Mom leaving a note on her door one morning. My sister, who was 6, read it to me. I was 5. It said our dog had got lost and Mom was looking for her. When she came home, Mom said our dog had been hit by a car and died instantly, and she was sure it hadn't hurt. I cried and hit her and ran to my room. That night I had dreams of cars hitting Bessie over and over. For days after that I wouldn't get in the car unless someone spanked me. After a while, I got used to Bessie not being there. But even now, I remember how it hurt. No one explained to me about death, but I wished they would have.

Our cat jumped into a yard and hit the electric fence and the dogs in the yard started dragging him around and he died. We all cried. I was eleven and didn't know all about death, but I knew he won't be back.

My neighbor called up and said that my dog Fritz had been hit by a car behind her house. I ran out to my dog. I was hysterical, crying, yelling. I was scared and sad. We buried him ourselves. My sister cut off some of his hair and gave it to me. We made a stone that said "We will always love you, Fritz."

We had this cat that followed me around everywhere I went. He didn't like my sister and was always scratching her. One day I woke up and he was really sick. My mother took him to the vet, but he had been bitten by a spider, so the vet put him to sleep. I remember the office smelt awful because the last patient had "gone" all over *the floor. When we left I kept screaming at my mother that she had forgot my cat.*

We had three hamsters altogether. Each one was called Herman. One died of pneumonia. Another died because of loneliness. The other one died when my Mom came in where we kept him. He was playing on his exercise wheel. When he saw my Mom, he stopped, but the exercise wheel didn't. He caught his foot or his neck. We took him to a small animal doctor, but he couldn't do anything. Since then, we haven't had another.

My Dad was digging a pool with a steam shovel. When his scoop on the shovel swung around, it hit my dog Boots. My Dad put him in my wagon and took him someplace and buried him. There were some bloodstains in my wagon and I never wanted to get in it again. The wagon got all rusty after that.

Often our adult impulse is to downplay the death of a pet. Many parents feel uncomfortable when kids are upset, angry, or depressed about the fate of an animal, so they try to explain the death away. "I talked to my Mom about it. She said he'll just go up to heaven and live again up there. I said, 'Oh! Then everything's OK.' And I went up to bed." "Mom said our dog had been hit by a car. She had died instantly and Mom said she was sure it didn't hurt." A mother or father will frequently replace the pet immediately with another like it. There is something right and healing about this, but not if it is a bribe to short-circuit the feelings of grief and loss. It's interesting that some children themselves have already internalized this diversionary technique to cut off feeling.

I was in my yard when a dog got run over. The dog was still alive when I got there. The dog's waste was lying in the sand. I knew then he was going to die. They took the dog to the vet. I told the little boy not to worry about it. I took him to see some little kittens to get his mind off his dog.

Sometimes kids feel guilty when their pets die.

Pebbles was our black Labrador retriever. My mother went downstairs and poured some Drano down a drain on the floor. She came up and told us not to let Pebbles downstairs. I went downstairs and forgot to shut the door and Pebbles came after me. She went right over to the place where my Mom had poured the Drano and just licked it all up. I was hitting her and shouting at the top of my voice. My mother came down and put Pebbles outside. She ate snow and from her mouth was a bunch of foam. We took her to the vet. The next day the vet called and said Pebbles was dead. I cried and wouldn't stop, and my brother was mad at me. He told me I killed Pebbles and that really made me cry! To this day I wonder if I did kill her.

It's been about ten months now since my dog died. Most of the time when I think about her, I get feelings of guilt. That's because we also have a collie that she hated. I like that collie very much. I spent much of my time training him and taking him for walks. I also used to feel guilty

IF I DIE & WHEN I DO

because I'd try to remember her clearly after her death, and I couldn't.

My cat Sugar got run over in front of our house about four years ago. Recently my other cat disappeared. I haven't seen him for three months. I cry a lot for both of my cats. Sometimes I feel I'll never stop crying and feel guilty about their deaths.

The first time I dealt with death was when my best friend died of cancer. Then my fishes, and then my great-grandmother, and then my cat — all in one month's time. Well, all I could feel was guilt. I thought everything I loved died. So I started hating everything until my Mother sat me down and explained the physical form of death and mixed some religion in. Like heaven and God. I was about seven years old.

In addition to generalized guilt feelings on the part of the children, there is a strong and very human need to pin responsibility on someone when a tragedy like the death of a loved pet occurs. Parents are often the ones who get the blame.

My parakeet, Peppy, was in a cage in the kitchen. It was a few days before Thanksgiving and my mother was doing something with onions. We knew Peppy was sick, and he refused to take the medicine the vet told us to give to him. He died about 7:30. I lost control of myself. I started blaming my Mom for cutting the onions. I thought that's what made him die.

My Dad backed over Froed.
He was my pet toad.
I felt very sad
and I blamed my Dad.
I was the one I should have blamed,
because I let him go.

The magic I felt in the classroom while we shared our personal journeys was in the transformation of our attitudes toward death. It became clear to me that the simple act of openly talking about those we loved, the death process, our fears and our losses, quickly brought us to a deeper acceptance of the place of death in life. At the very least, these young people entered the classroom anticipating that each session would hold something of value for them.

It is in the dark silence surrounding many children's early experiences with death that dread and fear thrive. Almost without exception, when one person had taken the time to be with a child in sadness and to share thoughts and feelings about death, the child experienced death as somehow appropriate to life.

I heard these young voices asking for straightforward information when a death occurred, for clear emotional sharing, and, mostly, for respect.

I was five years old when my mother's best friend was killed by an unknown assailant. My mom was walking around in a daze, amazed that a person she knew could really die. She couldn't explain to me about what was going on, so all I can remember is feeling left out of something important that I was supposed to cry about. I felt a sort of revenge, for this thing called death had taken my Mom away from me and had made her very sad.

IF I DIE & WHEN I DO

Exploring Beliefs about Death

3

"Life Is a Birthday Cake,
Death a Coffin"

Although homework assignments about topics related to death worked well for many students, I found myself wanting to provide them with more opportunities for immediate expression of their feelings, thoughts, and experiences. I wanted my classroom to be an alive and thriving place in which these young people could discover their own creativity.

Thanks to a timely suggestion from my own teacher and dear friend, Gay Hendricks, I introduced "Creative Energy Days." These were lively and colorful occasions. Into the classroom I would bring paints, crayons, paper of different colors and sizes, old magazines, glue, musical instruments, records, poetry, scissors, short stories. On three or four blackboards I put quotes, suggested topics for exploration, pictures, and questions. I told the students that they were free to do what they wanted with the materials and that they could use their own creative ideas to express feelings about death. After a time of getting used to this new atmosphere, students began exploring their own creative processes.

Some students seemed to have an unending flow of creative energy. Those who seemed to have lost touch with the imaginative part of themselves were slower to begin. Finally, they would burst out with, "What do you want me to *do*?" Some just sat quietly for five or ten minutes, and the next time I looked were intensely involved in writing or painting. A few spent time listening to music or talking with friends before getting down to work.

The walls of my room were portable and could be used as display areas from floor to ceiling. At the beginning of each course they were empty. By the end, they were filled. I was constantly surprised at the number of kids who came in from other classes just to catch up on the latest poems, stories, pictures, collages.

Some students took photographs or made movies. Others devised questionnaires to use in interviewing family or friends. For many, the first step was just to print out the taboo words having to do with death and color them large and bold. Here are some of the creations that appeared on our walls:

DEATH IS . . .

OLD AGE
DYING
AGONY
A GRAVEYARD
BLACK
STARTING A NEW WORLD
THE END OF A LIFE CHAIN
THE BEGINNING OF A NEW LIFE
RELIVING
GONE
SAD
STARTING ALL OVER

Gain all you can from each day, for death is not going to wait around for you to finish up.

DEATH
DREADFUL
EERIE
AWFUL
TERRIBLE
HORRIBLE

LIFE IS A ONE-WAY ROAD TO DEATH!

As students became more accustomed to acknowledging the presence of death in their lives, their creative responses expanded.

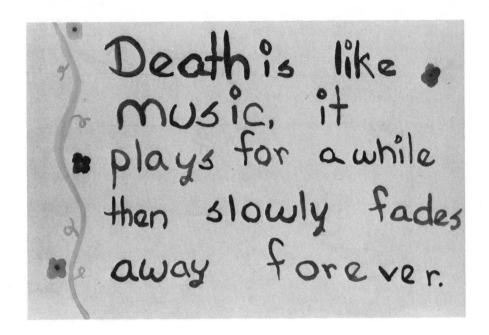

Death is like music, it plays for a while then slowly fades away forever.

The following were written largely in response to a request for expressions of "What Death Means to Me."

THE FLOWER OF DEATH

Death is like a flower
Wilting in the sun,
It can't live because
It has no-one.
If someone gave it love
It could rise above
And shine out light
All through the night
To kill the gloom
And make all the flowers BLOOM!

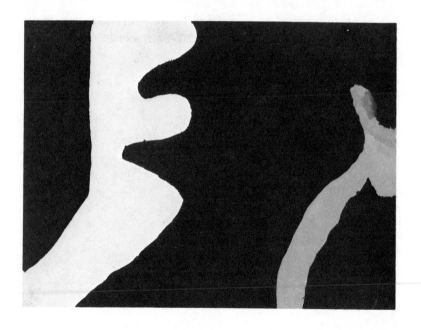

IF I DIE & WHEN I DO

DEATH THOUGHTS

Death makes me think of a day when nothing is going right, when you are all alone and feeling scared, when you are old and sitting in a rocking chair knitting a sweater because you have nothing else to do, or when you are having an operation and they put the gas mask on your face.

DEATH IS . . .

1. A ceasing of functioning of both body and mind
2. A fear so deep it is terrifying
3. A darkness of life
4. A very strong mental denial
5. A kind of mystery everyone has
6. Deep emotion which conquers most

THE DEATH CHILD

I think death is like having a child. You want to have your child, but you are afraid of the pain, and you wonder what life will be like for him.

THE UNKNOWN

Death is unknown to most everyone,
Daughter after daughter, son after son.

PARADOX

Death is wonderful yet frightening.
Death is harmless yet it hurts.
Death is the end, but you're just beginning.
Death is as dark as the black night
but as light as a burning sun.
Death is never-ending.

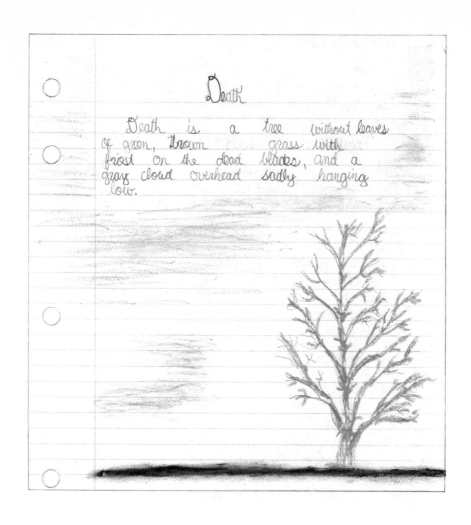

Death

Death is a tree without leaves of green, brown grass with frost on the dead blades, and a gray cloud overhead sadly hanging low.

DEATH IS . . .
Hope, it cures all sickness,
it relieves all pain,
it comes without a struggle,
it heals.

Haiku

Death

Sometimes death comes on slowly,
Coming creapy, Sneaky.
But, sometimes fast as lightning.

DEATH MASK

Her lips were drawn tight,
Her face was pale,
When you felt for a pulse
There was none.
Her hands held a chill,
Her fingers, once smooth,
Were skin stretched over bone.
When you looked at her eyes,
All bloodshot and grey,
There was no doubt in your mind.
She was none other than
Death Herself.

IF I DIE & WHEN I DO

THE LAST LOOK

One more peek, just one more!
He looks so calm, so peaceful,
It must be great, I see what's in store.

His eyes are closed, his body still
No more concern, no fear, no thrill.

I'll run to his box and put in a book
And so I'll get that one, last look.

A DEATH COUPLET

Death is sad, death is lonely,
I wish I could think of happiness only.

SALLY

Silly Sally,
Sadly crying,
Sadly dying,
Sweetly saying
Sorry, Sandy.

TWO WORDS

Death and dead. Death is such a calm, smooth word. It floats on a cloud. Dead is such a hard word. It just stops. It reminds me of black.

DEATH EXPLAINED

She told me about death
In her very last breath
As they lowered her down
Six feet in the ground.

GUESS

It happens to everyone
  large and small,
there's no escaping it
  no way at all.

It comes to the rich
  as well as the poor,
at its pestering knock
  you must open the door.

We make myths to comfort us
  from its crushing blow,
but we find out the truth
  when we must go.

You may guess what you wish,
  think what you think,
but death will come
  and into it you'll sink.

I WILL NEVER KNOW

Once upon a lifetime
A girl knew she was going to die.
Three months to live a lifetime, and
She asks the question, why?

The world will go on without me,
The seasons will come and go,
The sun will rise and set into the rolling sea,
And I will never know.

IF I DIE & WHEN I DO

FRIENDLESS DEATH

Death is going
Death is never coming back
Death has no friends
But always takes someone else's.

THE END AND THE BEGINNING

Life is knowing you're all there,
being able to love and care,
doing things you want to do
and caring for others around you.
For life is your beginning.

Death is a feeling of complete darkness,
People wish it less and less.
Death is a time of sorrow,
it may strike today or tomorrow.
For death is your ending.

DEATH quick, painless
LIFE melting, like icing on a cake

LIFE AND DEATH

Life is short and happy
Death is long and sad
Life is wished by all
Death is feared by all
Life is a new seed being born
Death is a leaf falling from a tree
Life is a birthday cake
Death a coffin.

Dealing with Fears of Death

"A Cold, Chilly Feeling"

One of the most important topics the students and I discussed during our sessions was fear. Together we explored our fears and became aware of how many were related to death. Dealing with feelings of fear—and indeed, with all feelings—was important, not only because talking about them often diminishes and even dissolves them, but also because children do not receive much permission to *feel* their feelings. Often adults try to talk children out of feeling sad, angry, scared, or troubled. This is probably because we as adults may be afraid of our own feelings, and also because our natural compassion may be heightened when we see a young person hurting.

Feelings, both negative and positive, flow from the same source, so to deny the negative emotions is to deny the positive ones, also. If we wish to become whole and to help our children become whole, we must develop a loving acceptance of all of life—both the negative and the positive.

Feelings run deep in us all, and when the students sensed that it was all right to deal with their feelings, they wrote about their emotions with astonishing power and maturity.

THINKING ABOUT SUICIDE

Sometimes I feel like committing suicide. But I know I don't mean it. Still, in the back of my head, I really do mean it. When I start thinking seriously about it, I think of all the things I would be missing. Then about my parents, and how they would feel. But, as if a devil was in me, I say, "Who cares about my parents or brother or relatives? Even my friends, for that matter?" I hate this feeling, because it's sad and scary. Usually, when I say I don't care about what my parents think if I die, it is because of them that I want to die. At the beginning of 7th grade my marks were pretty bad and I had problems. Now I am proud of myself because my grades are better and I'm really giving it a try.

PAIN

A new life comes, pain comes
You fall, pain comes
You love, pain comes
You dream, pain comes
You live, pain lives
You die, pain dies.

IF I COULD STOP THE WORLD

If only I could stop the world,
Stop all time and events,
Just stop the pain, the suffering,
Stop it from moving and changing,
I would hold it tightly in my hands
And rest it a while.
If only I could stop the world.

Death, mysterious
Creeping up on you, like clouds
Dark, always coming.

FUNNY?

Wouldn't it be funny to have a child,
a child all your own, who loves and adores you,
wouldn't it be funny for this child
to grow up and be afraid of you?
Wouldn't it be funny for this child to turn on you,
this child that you've loved so much,
this child you've protected and devoted your life to,
wouldn't it be funny for this child to hate you,
to leave, and never come back?
Wouldn't it be funny?
Not at all.

Dealing with Fears of Death

HAPPY DEATH, UNHAPPY LIFE

Death, death!
It is when everyone is dancing to music,
Nobody stops! Laughter! Peacefulness!
No-one to make you unhappy!

THE TERROR OF LIVING

The problem of death
Is the fear it contains,
Yet the terror of living
Is just as insane.

CHILDHOOD

Sometimes when I'm sad —
  I cry
Sometimes when I'm mad —
  I cry.
Sometimes when I'm glad —
  I cry
I see you crying now —
  and I cry.

TO DIE FAST

I hope to have a long life and a happy one, to live 'till I'm
114 and see the 300th birthday of our country. But how
its been going lately for me, I'm not sure. Well, it's been
bad because my grandfather died and my grandmother is
really sick. It really discourages me, and things will never
be the same. I would like to die fast so I will not have so
much pain.

The day is warm,
but I am cold;
There is a sun,
But I see rain;
It is morning
but I see darkness;
Everyone is happy,
but I feel pain.
The sky is blue,
but I see shadows;
The air is laughter,
I am filled with tears;
A song that's happy,
Mine is mourningful;
Alone beside the window,
I wished a friend was
near.

NO TURNING BACK

Birth comes like the wind
and runs through the breeze
but ends all too quickly
with a space and a blank.

Love turns to grief,
fairness to cheating,
but there isn't any
turning back.

ILLUSION

Happiness is just illusion
I can come to no conclusion
From the fact that life's so hard.

Somewhere beyond
Peace lies,
Somewhere above
the cloudy skies.

We were put on earth for a reason,
I've not yet found mine.
My time will come. I've already left
So much behind.

I have not found my purpose here,
But I feel it's not too far.
Tomorrow will bring a new day,
Yesterday another scar.

LIFE . . . WHAT'S IT ALL ABOUT?

This so-called "world" is so screwed up. Everyone hates everyone else and there's so much trouble. I don't think God planned it that way.

I don't want to have children. I wouldn't want to bring them up in such a place. It's called "Earth" but it's really a second Hell.

Why don't people want to do something about this "earth"? They are too worried about themselves. I wish I could change it, but me, I don't have the power.

Dealing with Fears of Death

ALONE

Alone . . .
All by myself . . .
No one to talk to . . .
Scared . . .
Scared of nothing . . .
Scared of everything . . .

Alone . . .
Up against the whole world . . .
All by myself . . .

Dream . . .
Dream of a different place . . .
No wars . . .
No quarrels . . .
Happiness . . .

Death . . .
Death was not a word . . .
Death was not there . . .
Murders were not committed . . .
All animals, plants, and people
Lived in total happiness.

RUN

Run, little child, for the fun is gone.
Run, little child, for fear of the gun.
Run, not for fun, but for fear of your life.
Run, little child, for there is no light.

Young people are human beings, striving to fashion a viable self with which to cope with an immensely complex and stressful world. We do them no service when we, out of our fear or misguided compassion, fail to encourage them to experience the entire range of their feelings and thoughts.

Fear of the unknown was one of the primary student reactions to thoughts of dying. Another common fear was *how* death would come.

I think the first time I had anything to do with death was one night (I was about four) when I was in bed. I don't know, but I found myself to be thinking about death. I realized that I would die someday, and I cried and cried. I don't know if I thought that it would happen soon, just that in my mind I kept picturing my family all crying. That made me cry more.

All my life I've been afraid of death. It really scares me to think of lying still, dead, not thinking about anything. Whenever anyone speaks about someone who has died, or anything that has to do with death, it scares me and makes me feel sick. I have many fears but I think death is one of my worst.

Personally, I know I'd be terrified to die,
Losing everything I guess is the reason why,
Wondering where you'll end up,
Perhaps in a world of pain and corrupt,
Or maybe with everything you could ever want,
Not having to hunt for something beautiful.

A HALLWAY FULL OF FIRE AND FLAME

A hallway full
of fire and flame,
looking for someone
I can blame.

My feet won't do
what I want them to
I'm paralysed
from head to toe.

My mouth doesn't do
what it should do,
it's closed with your hand
that covers my face.
Bull black and frightening,
what a horrible place!

A hallway full
of fire and flame,
the very point
from whence I came!

I can't quite remember who told me about death. But I remember a stage in my life when I thought life was super-short. I was embarrassed to talk to my grandparents because I thought every word I said would make them feel uncomfortable, knowing that I was going to live longer than they were. I remember thinking that I had to prepare myself for my grandparents' death every day, and I thought that I would die soon after my grandparents did.

After maybe a year, that stage of my life settled down a bit. But for the next two or three years, every time I hurt myself or tasted something funny, I thought, "This is the end!" When I was around 6, I swallowed a BB pellet. Every day that went by, I was surprised that I was still alive. Well, I suppose I didn't die on account of that BB, because here I am today, in a stage of wondering and concern about death.

GLOOMY DEATH

Death, death, makes things collapse.
Death makes things dark and gloomy.
I hate death.
Death is all a terrible dream.

A COLD, CHILLY FEELING

*Death is a cold, chilly feeling
When you don't know what is in store.
You may live until tomorrow
But you may live much more.*

*Death is that cold, chilly feeling you get
When you drive past a graveyard at night,
For they are dead and you don't know why,
That's what causes the fright.*

*Death is your cold, chilly feeling
When you stare into his coffin,
For it doesn't happen
All that often.*

WHAT WOULD BE THE WORST WAY
FOR ME TO DIE?

*1. Suffocation — because I have asthma, and suffocation
reminds me of it.
2. Choking — because my asthma reminds me of choking and my neck is just fragile.
3. Suicide — because I don't like to think of what would
make me do it.
4. Stabbed — I don't like blood and I think it would be
worse for my family, and it would leave hatred for the
killer.
5. Cancer — because usually you suffer longer.
6. Shot — because people say you cannot feel shots.
7. Natural death — I'm undecided if a natural death is
good or bad.*

*In all I'm not very afraid to "die" but I'm more afraid of
how I'm going to die.*

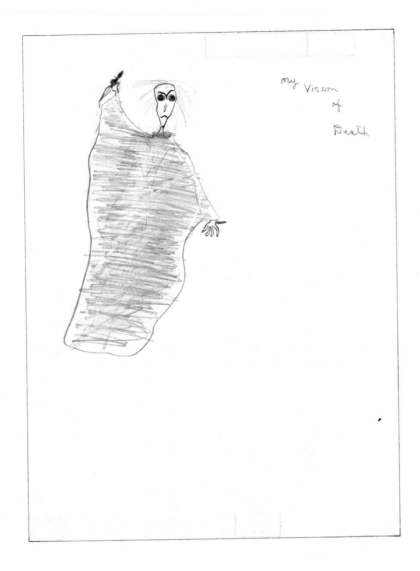

My Vision
of
Death

IF I HAVE TO GO SOON

If I have to go soon
I want to go when there is peace,
Not when there is war, or when
There is hate.
If I have to go soon
I want to go in peace, in sleep,
Without struggle.
If I have to go soon,
I want to go easy.

*The reason I am scared of death is because I don't want
to die suffering. I hate car accidents because I am always
thinking that I will end up in the hospital. I just hate going
to the hospital or doctor.*

**In our class, some students confronted the futility of
life. What can it be worth if it all has to end in death?**

Death is like autumn.
First the trees turn golden brown
and orange and yellow.
They are beautiful,
so are people

Trees die,
so do people.

But trees come back to life.
People don't.

Life is climbing, climbing a tree . . .
Death is slipping on a limb
and falling, falling, falling,
hitting the ground . . .
It's all over.

Some kids used their vivid imaginations to make a journey to the time of their own death.

WHO, ME?

Life is so beautiful
the birds and the bees
the wonderful mountains
the sun and the seas.
But when you must die,
the thought is so painful.
Where is the beauty?
It's all faded away.
You're in such depression,
the world is so grey.
You're fighting and fighting,
it can't be true!
You're not dying,
it can't be you!

For a few students, fears of death were associated with concerns far beyond the personal. To one who passionately loved the mountain forests, death brought an immediate image of careless people and devastating forest fires. Another felt, "Yet I'm sorta glad that I will die. If I had everlasting youth that would mean I would live forever in this air of pollution." Yet another associated death with the constant escalation of war.

I think that today we have a different attitude towards death than ever before. In the past we have always had at least some temporary control over our deaths, such as, "Don't break the law and you won't get shot!" "Be careful and you may not get diseases," and other preventatives. Though we still have these and more, thanks to medical science, we now have a new threat: nuclear weapons and nuclear fall-out. Because of these, the entire world's population could be wiped out in less than 10 minutes. If someone in a foreign country pushed a button or pulled a lever they could kill you and all your friends, from thousands of miles away, in one and a half minutes. However, maybe there's a good side to this too. Perhaps now the cost is finally too high, perhaps now there will be no more major wars. Let us hope.

But fears associated with death were personal for most of the students — fears of the pain associated with dying, of loss and loneliness, of somehow being able to sense the terror of not being. A few students had strong reactions to discussing death. When I thought it appropriate, I invited counselors, social workers, and parents to come together to work with these children.

What we all came to realize was that everyone has fears and that there is no shame in this.

A graveyard can really shake me up. There is one in Kansas City, Missouri that bugs me the most. My Grandpa died when I was two, and we go to visit his grave every year. This year, I found out something that caught me off guard. My parents own two lots next to him.

I was forced to think about the fact that my parents will die sometime, and will be held prisoner in a cold, hard, small cage enclosed by lifeless soil. Never being able to move. Captured by fate. I started to cry for us all, all the living. When we die there is no freedom. No movement. No nothing.

Humor & Death

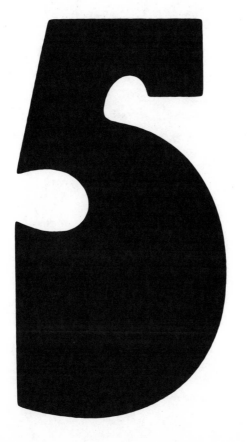

"Once You're Dead,
Life Isn't Worth Living"

We laughed a lot, too, in those death classes. It was, truly, a major part of the teaching. After being with the students for a while, I found my own inner child emerging. There was one particularly rowdy class. Sometimes I would sneak along the wall and peer into the room where they were gathering before the class. Quickly, some students would sneak along the corresponding wall and we would all jump out at each other, screaming and laughing our way into the beginning of another session.

Each one of us has our own rhythm in life. A group of people also has a rhythm. I began to acknowledge this and to let go of my adult need to be in control of the situation. The beginning of most classes became a fluid, dynamic time when students meandered around — some talking with other students, others sharing stories, concerns, or jokes with me. I was often surprised at how gently the group settled itself into readiness for the day's activities.

There is something absurd about the statement I often heard when I was a kid: "Grow up! Quit acting like a child!" I found that it was in respecting *all* parts of young people—especially their childlike parts—that I could get them to share their deeper, wiser selves with me.

For example, I had a little pocket calculator that sat on my desk during the class. I found myself picking up the calculator one day, looking at it, pushing a few random buttons, putting the machine to my ear, and then talking into it. I looked up and found all eyes upon me. It struck me then how rare it was for these kids to see an adult acting silly. After this incident, I would frequently walk into the classroom when a student was playing with the calculator. He or she would look up and see me, hand me the machine, and say, "Here—someone wants to talk to you."

Although little of this humor was written down, I think it is important to acknowledge how helpful it was in letting us grow close to one another.

Junior high kids are endlessly and exasperatingly funny. In dealing with death, a subject that evokes so much emotion, I found it essential to allow humor to bubble up freely. Like grief, laughter can be cleansing and rejuvenating, a gift to oneself and others.

For example, one student asked her mother if she had thought about what kind of funeral arrangements she wanted when she died. Her mother said, "I don't care. I'll be dead!" Of herself, the student wrote: "I want to be buried underground. Why, I really don't know except, for one thing, I wouldn't want ashes on *my* fireplace, so I think no one would want my ashes on *their* fireplace."

Sometimes the daily newspaper provided the material for the kind of grisly humor that has a special appeal to 13- and 14-year-olds.

On the news I heard about a family who recently moved to the U.S. from Italy. They received a box in the mail from Argentina. It came without a letter, and they thought a good friend had sent spices. They used the spices for

*about two weeks, then received this belated letter: "We
are shipping you your grandmother's ashes."*

**This, needless to say, was headlined "They Ate Their
Grandmother."**
**Some kids seem to have a particular knack for dead-
pan, brave, macabre wit.**

*If you get shot
you might rot.*

*If you get strangled
you might look mangled.*

*I hope I don't die till I'm old
So I won't mold.*

*When I die bury me deep
Plant some roses at my feet
Around my head the maggots will creep
It won't bother me, I'll be asleep!*

*I like death, death likes me.
Oh, my Gosh, my Golly Gee!
Death is nice, nicer than spice,
It's the way we're meant to be!*

*If you think failing's bad
Wait till you die, that's pretty sad!*

*Don't think of life as a cheap shot
Think of it so it will mean a lot.*

One young person summed up the link between humor and human nature beautifully in two lines:

Sometimes I laugh when I feel like crying,
Sometimes I smile when I feel like dying.

Life is a dread
When you're in bed,
But when you die
People start to cry.
When they think of death
People lose their breath.
It's like when you win
Death is deep within.
Although death is sorrow,
They'll forget tomorrow.

Skipping rope can skin a knee
And injury come from a falling tree,
but it's no joke
when they say I'll croak.

Sometimes the humor is unintentional. One boy, writing on the topic of how he would like to die, came up with, "I think I would probably like to die in an electric chair because it is the quickest and almost has no pain at all, except at the beginning, so I would not suffer as much as in a slow death." And one girl, holding an interview with her 8-year-old brother, asked him, "Are you afraid to die?" He responded, "Yes, because I've never died before." Another student contemplated donating his body to science after he died, saying, "I would donate my body to science as long as I have been proved clinically dead for one week." Trying to decide how she would like to have her body disposed of, a girl said she would "rather be creamated than berried." Another, describing the death of a friend, told how "he fell into a comma and died." One response to an assignment to relate how you would tell a child about death:

Explaining death to a kid
is not a piece of pie,
Because you gotta be there to know
just how it is to die!

And what about the perspective on age that is contained in the following?

I'd like to die when I was about 45. I picked this age because I'd still be able to get around without being in a nursing home. Also, people don't really pity you at that age and I hate people who pity me!

Last night I dreamed that I looked like an old lady with wrinkles and grey hair. They stuck me in a nursing home and made me play bingo all the time.

By laughing about death, we learned to laugh more in life. Without humor, any subject I taught would have died.

Learning to Ask the Big Questions

"Why Does Everyone Come and Go?"

When I talked with my students about life and death, one thing came as somewhat of a shock. The basic, major questions were exactly the same for them as for me. As we get older, we use longer words to describe our mystification, our sense of frustration, our hunger for answers. But the fundamental, gnawing, unanswerable questions surface early and remain to shape our lives.

I found myself encouraging students to turn in questions as much as any other kind of work. We used one whole wall as a Question Wall. When a question could be answered it was taken down to make room for one that did not yet have an available answer. Eventually there were questions all over the room — and hanging from the ceiling, too.

The Big Questions: What is life? What is death? Why do we die? Why is there suffering and pain in the world? Who do some people die young? Is there any meaning or purpose to the endless cycle of living and dying? What happens after death? Who am I? What am I?

As one young person wrote,

Death haunts me
As I sit quivering in wonder
Why, I ask, why is Death?
And the Answer comes back,
Slowly,
Death is for the dying.

Some kids ask simply and forthrightly:

To die. How, and why?
I will not lie
For I don't know why,
But I'd so hate to die
Without telling you why.

Why am I here
If there are things for me to fear?
Why do things stay alive
Until they die, and not survive?
Why are you, you,
And me, me, instead of a
Soft, yellow dew?

To me death
Is always there,
Causing me to ask
Why, when and where?

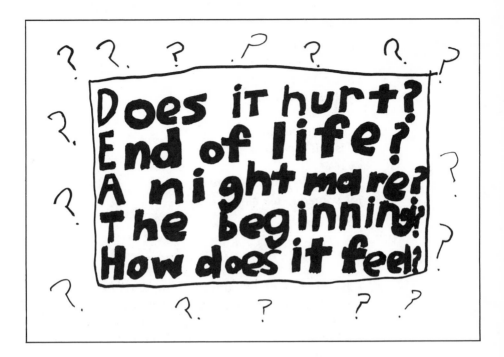

Is it bitter, is it sweet,
The darkness that we meet?
How do we meet this new shore?
Yes, it is death's door.

Life to me is very questionable. There are so many questions, and most we can't understand or they are unanswerable. Life is interesting and most people live it long. But there are some unfortunate people that live it short. Life can be terrible or wonderful. One of my biggest questions about life, if it does turn out wonderful, would probably be, "Why does it end?"

When we die
are we dead?

Or are we starting
a whole new life?

Is this life better,
or is this life worse?

We wonder, but not forever,
for someday we all will die.

I think I will look forward to death, it will be a big experi-
ence. Even before this class, I always wondered what it
would be like to be dead. Do you go to heaven, or just
die? One thing that really bewildered me is what it would
feel like to be dead. Are you just dead, or really alive?

Is death night or day?
Is living bright and sunny
Or dark and gray?
Is death the beginning or the end?
Is life good and death bad,
Or death good and life bad?
Is there a heaven or hell?
I wish I knew, I cannot tell.
But maybe,
Life is partly good and partly bad,
And death is the same.

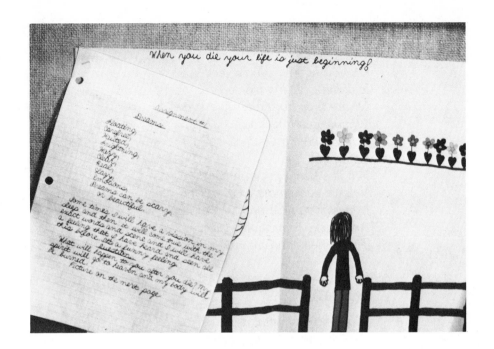

LIFE AND DEATH

Life, what is it?
Life is just a shadow
that passes you by.
Life is just happiness,
love, hope and fear.
Life is the beginning of death.

Death, what is it?
Death is just a fear
that goes through everybody.
Death is the end of life.

WILL WE EVER KNOW?

When death is near,
Do you have a special fear?
Is death or aging worse?
Or are they both a terrible curse?
What is death to you?
Is it something you just do?
When you age
Is it like being put in a cage:
Will we ever know what death is?
I guess not, till it happens to Liz
And Jack, John, Sally, Nancy, Joe
Tina, Shelly and me and you.

IS DEATH . . .

Is death as frightful as it really seems
Or is it part of imaginary dreams?

Does death seem pleasant or sad,
Or maybe even good or bad?

Will I be rich or poor
When death comes knocking at my door?

To some young people, the questions raise themselves in subtle form and are reflected in beautiful and haunting phrases.

What is death?
A toy to play with?
Or is it a pillow to lay your head on?
Is it nice and soft, or hard and cold?
What is death? Who really knows?

Death.

What is death?

Is it a green pasture?

A happy place?

A reunion of friends and family?

A dark room?

A quiet, sad place?

A beginning?

A reflection on our lives?

Is it something that just disposes of us?

Is death just a simple process, a person's body stops functioning, no longer smiling, happy or laughing?

People come to the funeral, cry a little or cry a lot.

People feel guilty at death, feel burdened with sadness, but then slowly and surely it is forgotten.

No longer sad and crying, no more burdens. Life goes on.

But is death really sad? Maybe its a joyous place where everyone is smiling, meeting friends and loved ones.

Everybody laughing down at the ones who are crying over their deaths.

Laughing at the people who don't know the happiness death causes.

Laughing. Laughing.

Is death bright and happy?

Only time will tell.

TO PLAY, TO DIE

Life is beautiful.
To sing, to laugh,
To sigh, to work,
To play . . . to die!
Why do we die?

*Do I really know where I stand on the subject of death?
Do I have my thoughts and beliefs all packaged up and
stored in a neat, organized corner of my mind? I thought
for sure I had it together, but I'm having second thoughts
now.*

*Why do we get old and die?
Why should we be sad and cry?
Why can't we be happy and gay
Even if we cannot stay?*

*Why do tears flow from the eye?
Why is it so sad to die?
I ask these questions, I'd like to know
Why does everyone come and go?*

Old Age
& Death

"While Rivers Flow,
Your Hair Turns Gray"

Old
Are they afraid?
Why do we hate them?
Silence.

When young, you hope you will never grow old.
When you look at someone who is old
You think of them as death, the end.

Old age does not evoke many positive images in junior high students. In this, perhaps more than any other single area, they reflect the culture that produced them, a culture that does not see the value of aging.

When was the last time you thought about getting old
When you're lonely, stiff, sore and cold?

Now, you can't imagine getting old,
But sooner than you think, you'll begin to fold.

You'll look back and think how you were,
So carefree, not worrying about feeling insecure.

So live your glory,
Soon you'll be history.

A man walks down the street and tries to talk to people,
but no one listens to him. The man is old and dying of
lonesomeness. He dies and nobody knows about it. He
dies along with his name.

I see old people shuffling down the lane
And I sometimes wonder, what is pain?

I realize that spring has sprung
And senior citizens wish they were young.

I wonder why old is a dreaded thing?
Why do I ponder this in spring?

I see a wrinkled, shriveled man
Walk past a track where he once ran.

Death makes me think of dark, ugly, lonely days.
That's why I don't want to die.
Well, I don't really mind dying, but growing old.
I don't want to die lonely.

The pictures evoked by old age were the results of simple exercises: Imagine yourself at the age of 75 —

What are you like?

How do you spend your time?

What do you live on?

Whom do you see?

Make a list of characteristics that come to your mind when you think of old age.

Besides visual pictures, the students also contributed poignant portraits in words.

Bony

Wrinkly

No one to care for them

Weak

Lonely

Sorta helpless at times

Gray hair

Whenever I think of myself being old, I picture an old woman sitting on a porch and in a rocking chair with a long dress and a shawl. I look really wrinkled and lonely. I don't like to think about it because it makes me sad. I'm sort of prejudiced against old people.

To me, aging seems like when you were a baby and you depend on everyone until you learned how to be independent for a while. Then, as you get older, you go back and depend on everyone again.

My Grandma used to be a considerate person who did a lot for others, but ever since my Grandpa died she has closed up. She hardly ever goes out and she thinks about herself all the time. She thinks she can't do anything. Sometimes she thinks she is sick when she's not. I like my Grandma, but I wouldn't like to be like her.

The house was dark
as the old grandma
sat in her chair
sleeping, dreaming of days long gone,
of her dead husband John,
of children grown so long,
of happy moments long ago.

A sudden deep breath.
A creak as the chair stops.

No one there
to comfort her,
no one to care,
or stroke her hair.

A lonely old woman
alone in the house
and no one knows,
no, no one knows.

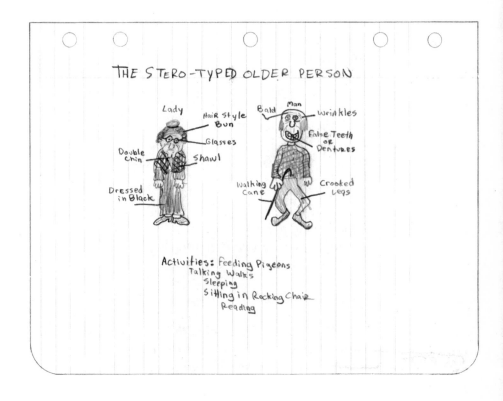

I don't want to get old. It scares me. I know that I will have millions of wrinkles because my skin is so dry and I already have a lot. I think I'll be short and skinny and bent over and I will look very old. I'm afraid of getting old because people will pity me, and they won't understand that I was young once and active and I was just as smart as they are. I'm afraid I'll be so dependent on everyone. I'll be at the end of life looking back, instead of at the beginning looking forward.

When I think of aging
It reminds me of wrinkling skin.
I know it happens naturally,
So it sure can't be a sin.

Next I think of walking,
Walking oh! so slow,
Your bones are just so weak
All the bones from head to toe.

Then there are the people
Who will make fun of you,
Every day you walk by them
They make a joke or two.

Last of all there's dying,
A frightening thing to me,
Wondering where you're gonna go
What you'll turn out to be.

I am 75 years old. I have grayish hair, wrinkly skin, and I am very thin. I wear pearls and red lipstick. I am weak, and there is only a small resemblance to what I used to look like. I'm living in an old house on a lonely street of old people. The house is run-down and needs painting badly. My husband has died. I don't work because I am weak and have no qualifications. I just stay home and take care of myself. When I get up in the morning, I go down and put on a kettle. I let the dog out. I have tea and toast. Then I look at magazines and watch TV until lunch. Then I have a sandwich and lie down. At dinner, I heat a frozen dinner, watch more TV in the evening. What I enjoy is watching children play. What makes me sad is seeing people ruin things. If I could change one thing, I'd like to have a lot of energy.

My great-grandfather died at the age of ninety. But for a long time he was as good as dead anyway, for he would not change. He would never go out of the house and he could not accept the present. His biggest grudge was that he did not believe that men could fly to the moon. He thought it was all a hoax.

As children of their time, students placed an inordinate value on youth and on all the physical attributes and activities youth implies. Where youth is an absolute value, old age seems to be bearable only if as many youthful characteristics as possible are retained.

At 75 I look very young for my age and I have been trying to keep in shape. I have gray hair and wrinkly skin. I live in a high-class apartment complex with a foxy old woman the same age as I who is very young-looking and groovy. I'm living on a very, very big pension. In the morning I get out of my waterbed and pull some eggs out of my microwave for breakfast. I get dressed, hop in my Jag and go play golf. Then to the spa for a couple of hours. I take my chick to my favorite French restaurant for dinner, then home to a fire and a read before bed.

Whenever I try to picture myself as an old woman, I think of pictures in movies or commercials. I guess I don't want to be old. I want to be pretty and skinny and in shape. I don't want to be fat and ugly.

MY GRANDMA AND GRANDPA

My Grandma is real nice. I think she is about 68. She really likes to travel. For her 40th anniversary, they went on a 4 week trip to the Orient. She just went to Russia before Christmas. My Grandpa plays golf and likes to fish. They go to the ocean a lot. They live in a big house that isn't old. I don't think they are like most old people.

So, like many of us, kids have a double-bind thought process that guarantees negative images of aging. If people are old in years, but healthy, vigorous, independent, and enjoying life, then they are "not like most old people." And all the sad, sick, dependent examples of old people they see reinforce their terrors of growing old. The positive examples are an atypical few who just haven't become old yet.

In the students' written efforts there were a few examples of older relatives who did not match the stereotypical role of giving their life over to an institution until they died.

My aunt was 84 when she broke her hip. She was the most wonderful woman I ever met. She did not really care that she was old, she still had more fun than a teen-

ager. She had a snappy answer to any question you could ask. She broke her hip on a Tuesday. On Wednesday I went to see her. That was the last time I saw her alive. She was still smiling, even through the pain. Friday my Dad told her she would have to go into a home when she got better. She yelled and screamed, and then she cried. Saturday she was dead. The doctors told us she had taken the I.V.'s out during the night. I wish you could have met her. She was some lady.

Those whom students perceived as typically "old" embodied the tragic side of old age — sickness, loss of mental and physical powers, and dependence. Many had seen these aspects of age as their own older relatives grew infirm.

My Grandma is a very old and sick woman. She lives all alone in an old house. She's blind, too. Her house is a dangerous fire hazard. My uncles and aunts want her to go to a nursing home, but she doesn't want to. She's fallen down the stairs a few times and really hurt herself. She just got out of the hospital from a stroke. Before that, she had a heart attack. They found a really nice place for old people, more like apartments than a nursing home. My uncles and aunts were going to pay for some of it, too. But she doesn't want to move. She's lived in her house almost all of her life and doesn't want to leave it. Pretty soon she's going to die. I think she should go and live in those apartments. She might live a little longer.

When my grandfather was dying he was put in a nursing home. He was treated like a baby because he had had three or four strokes and his brain wasn't normal. He played with little rattles for babies, and he wet the bed. He couldn't help it, but the nurses still treated him cruelly. After about his 6th stroke, he was really badly off. He was almost like a vegetable until he died after his 7th stroke. My mother was glad to get him out of the misery, but my Grandmother was all upset and mourned for months.

Grandma had always been sick and had had several strokes. I can remember most clearly a visit we paid her before they put her on a machine to keep her alive. She couldn't talk and could hardly move, let alone hear us. We brought her some flowers and I stood up on a stool so she could see me. I remember her smiling at me and I could see by her eyes that she knew who I was. Then one night, a long time after they had plugged her in, my Mom woke me up and told me Grandma had died. She said they had turned off the machine because she was so miserable and that she wasn't going to hurt anymore.

One boy wrote a poignant life story of his great-grandmother, born in 1885. When she was young, her uncles told her stories of the Civil War. She was married twice, and both of her husbands were killed in accidents. She had two daughters and supported herself by dressmaking.

She was in her teens when the first car was driven, and she was a young woman when the first plane was flown. She has seen sixteen presidents come and go, and she has lived through five wars. She saw the coming of movies, from silent black and white to colored talkies, and she was already middle-aged when penicillin and the Salk vaccine came out.

Nana is now in a rest home and it seems to really be rough on her and everyone else. She can hardly hear, walk or see, and we think that she won't be with us much longer.

Yesterday, my Grandmother went into a nursing home. She had been staying at our house for the past week. She has hardening of the arteries and is always confused. She doesn't know where she is. She cannot remember our names, sometimes not even her own name. She is tiny and sweet, only weighs 85 lbs. I wanted to go with my Mom to take her to the nursing home, but my Mom wouldn't let me. The last time she went into the hospital, for some tests, and I went with them, Grandmother got really upset. She started hitting everyone and kept saying, "No, this isn't mine." about the hospital. When we left she said something really sad, "Girls, girls, don't leave me, I'm dying." I think maybe she'll be happier at the nursing home because there will probably be someone there with nothing but time to listen to her not make any sense. I do wish she could be the way she used to be.

Every time I go to visit my Grandma in the nursing home it's scary because we go and sit in the lounge and she doesn't say anything but, "Leave!" I don't understand, all the other people there are so friendly, except her. She has a disease which is all the veins from her body to her brain are getting smaller every day. She can't open her hands, and when my Dad tries to open them, she moves away. I want to help her, but how?

Most students had a pretty sad view of ending life in a nursing home.

One day, near Christmas, my church youth group went carolling at a nursing home. All the people there looked so lonely. They just sat in chairs staring out the window. It gave me the feeling they were waiting for death. Some of them started crying, and I wanted to stay there all day just so they would not be lonely. I felt awful because we only sang one or two songs and then moved on. I will always remember the looks on their faces, as if the world had forgotten them.

During the course, students listened to speakers familiar with both the problems and the assets of the elderly, watched thought-provoking films, read and talked out some of their own contradictory feelings about old age from new angles. This modified the outlook of many of them, at least temporarily. Basically fair-minded and compassionate, they looked for ways to reconcile their stereotyped, compartmentalized ideas and feelings about old people with new sensitivities and concepts.

Aging is a kind of sad thing and a happy feeling. The sad thing is you're not getting younger and people don't pay as much attention as they used to. They don't come visit you, you just stay home and cry.

Happy things are that you can do things on your own and you can take trips and collect things and you have an unforgettable past and you have a few who love and cherish you.

Aging is not only dark days and lonely times
Aging is also your golden years.
I am trying to overpower my fears.

More than once, I've been told I'm getting old,
I look back at life: it's not so bad,
I was happy and seldom sad.
I know I will leave one day
With happiness, in a special way.
If I had to live it over, I'd live it the same
But I know I can't, it's just a game.
I'm getting to where I'm ready to leave now,
Don't ask me why this is, or how.
Soon I will die
I'm ready to say . . . Good-bye!

TIME

As time goes on, at last
We have to understand,
Think of the future, not the past —
Movies, rollerskating, even Elton's band —
Move forward, don't look back
The times are changing rapidly
As you can clearly see,
Generations go by and by.
People born, people die,
Wedding bells, church chimes
In this world times change
And we must change with time.

GOD BLESS OLD PEOPLE—THEY'RE HUMANS TOO!

GRANDPAS

Grandpas are fun to talk to
They get a little older, a little wiser,
Telling tales of the past,
Wondering why it went so fast.

Sitting in the rocking chair
Thinking of his wife, what a pair!
Taking a walk in the park,
Coming in just before dark,
Having such good times.

But those times have to end,
He knows he's rounded the bend.
Maybe it's better that way.
Everyone has to die, some day.

Old people are pushed out of the world just like they
don't exist.

Wisdom is often seen as a valuable quality in the elderly, but not by junior high students. There seem to be no characteristics of the old that kids find admirable, or that they look forward to acquiring. There was a generalized belief among many of the students that growth in any form ended at about age 50. Many were genuinely afraid of aging.

In class we discussed the mythical nature of many of the stereotypes of aging. We read articles discussing research into sexuality, intelligence, physical abilities, and other human attributes as they relate to aging.

I still sensed a dread of aging in the students. There is a great deal to be done if people are to begin living during their aging years. I think now that the work must begin with very young children and their belief systems about life processes such as aging and dying.

The wind will blow
and trees will sway.
While rivers flow
Your hair turns gray.

Exploring What Happens after Death

*"A Life Beyond Life
That Is a Question"*

Students can express a variety of penetrating ideas and questions about death and dying. I saw this particularly in our sessions dealing with the possibilities of life after death. The questions about what happens after death were already being pondered by these young people.

Sometimes I really try to think what it would be like to die, but I never have come up with anything.

I've never had anyone close to me die, so I do not know how I would take it. I never imagined myself dead, or how my friends would react if I died. I really don't know how to deal with death at all.

Some stoically faced the idea that death was the end. Others contemplated it uneasily.

I think that when I die I'll just lay in my coffin and rot away, with no reincarnation, no life after death, no heaven, no hell, no floating, no sudden surge of happiness or sadness.

After the funeral I heard my cousin talking to a friend on the phone. He said something that scared me then and will probably bother me the rest of my life. "What if nothing happens when you die? What if you just stay in the ground until the earth stops turning?"

Most of the young people believed in some form of afterlife. Sometimes the belief was in the conventional idea of heaven and hell, with entry determined by behavior in this life.

I believe very strongly in life after death. I believe that in the end people will either go to heaven or hell. In my religion we believe that someday soon, or in the future, the Lord will come back. To prove this fact we have "Revelations" in the Bible. People can make their own decision to go to heaven or hell. I personally have accepted the Lord and believe that I am going to heaven.

OVER THE HILL

One step over the hill, it's green
Two steps over the hill, you feel keen
Three steps over the hill it's great
Four steps over the hill you've got the bait
Five steps over the hill, you're half way there
Six steps over the hill, you're in the air

Seven steps over the hill, the angels sing
Eight steps over the hill, the church bells ring
Nine steps over the hill, you see God's open hands
Ten steps over the hill, you can't believe where you
     stand.

Death is like a sin,
it does not end.
We all must die
and say good-bye.
They place the body in a casket
that looks like a large basket,
the body is dead.
But it has been said
the soul is with God
for a new beginning.
I think this is really winning.

**But the idea of hell seemed to be losing its grip on the
kids. Very few of the students — even the most religious
ones — accepted its reality.**

*When people have died, and are brought back to life,
they all say it's just gorgeous. But, no one has ever described hell. Why? Some people have to go to hell.*

*I don't believe that hell is a fiery furnace, but that not
going to heaven would be hell enough. I don't think you
are judged after you die, but if your soul is light enough
with love and forgiveness, you will go to heaven.*

The way I see it, you die at an age God has set out for you. Maybe it's at 2 years old or 92, but I think everyone leads one life and not two or three. I don't think there's a hell — I mean, everyone does something good at least once!

For some kids, junior high is the time when they begin to question parental and religious authority. This questioning includes beliefs about what happens after death.

When I die it's going to be one of my happiest and most exciting days. I don't know what's awaiting me after death. Within my mind, my parents and priest have almost made me believe that there is a heaven and a hell, and, without question, a God and a Devil. Still, I'm not totally convinced that there is a God. After all, I've never seen, touched or heard him. The only God I know is the one people have imprinted on my mind.

My religion has always made me believe that there is life after death and that I will go to heaven. From that belief I've built my own. For instance, I've always thought that if you were in heaven you could see the whole world. Or that you could live your whole life again. Or maybe you could be with the people you loved, without them seeing or knowing you were there.

A few raised the possibility that what happens after death may be structured by what one believes is going to happen.

I think that after I die, nothing will happen. Something might happen if you really believe in heaven or hell. You might go to one of them.

Heaven was sometimes thought of as a place where wishes and dreams came true.

I think of heaven as ten times better than earth, the mountains huge — ten times taller than they are here. There will be streets paved with gold and clean, clear streams.

I believe in a kind of heaven that would be like paradise. Everything would be perfect, nothing could go wrong. It would be beautiful, with no smog or pollution. No one could run my life. I would be free to go where I like with no one telling me what to do.

Perhaps the most characteristic reaction to the question of what happens after death was the expression of a semi-mystical perception of an afterlife as something that is not known, but an intuition of continuity.

LIFE IS LIKE
A STAIRWAY—

With all its trials and tribulations
When you get to the top, and die,
There's a whole second floor
to explore

— After you die — you go up there, and you see it all
before you — what you have done, where you have
gone, and what you now can do, and where you can go.
It's white for a while, then you're where you think you
want to be. I think that's why you can sometimes say,
"I've done this before" or "I've been here before" and
you know you haven't.

Or — after you die it is as it was. Nothing has happened.
You're still here young, just as you left off. The only
reason you died is to punish the others. But, they're still
there just as always, only you're in another place. This
must be heaven.

Is Death a box lined with silk material?
Is it crying, mourning, dressed in black?
Is it cold, lightning and pouring rain?
Is it eerie organ music in a dark room?
Is death forbidden, not allowed to happen?
Is it sad, grotesque, horrifying?
Is that what death is?

Or, is death a new beginning
As a flower revives in spring,
Is it a moist leaf just opening?
Or is it a beautiful sunset, all orange and yellow?

Death is a strong breeze stopping, a flower
going to sleep for the winter.
Death is another word for beginning, not ending.

The light goes out.
Your friends are gone.
But the loved ones that have
passed on long before you,
you meet again
in your place of paradise.
Even though you may be gone
from others still alive,
you will celebrate in seeing
the others long since gone.
Yet you will not forget
the life you lived.

Old things can never be recovered,
but do not worry.
You are in paradise.
Remembering them will not hurt you.
So be happy for death
to come in its time.
You are still alive.

In class we shared theories and beliefs about what comes after death, and we discussed what can be learned from talking with people who are dying and those who have had near-death experiences. We read Dr. Kübler-Ross's pioneer studies, Raymond Moody's *Life After Life,* and many similar books and articles. The students were tremendously interested in this area of discussion. Some related personal experiences and wrote stories incorporating some of their thoughts.

My Grandmother was dying of cancer. Her sister was sitting with her. Suddenly, her sister saw a big smile on my Grandmother's face and right after that, she died. I think the reason for the smile was because she saw my Grandfather waiting for her, and she was glad to see him and felt she was in good hands.

My father had a heart attack. When the nurses were taking him upstairs, his heart stopped. My Dad says he remembers only that it was very bright and that someone kept calling him. The doctor told us that he did die, but the nurses were able to get his heart beating again.

My parents had a friend at church who had "died" for quite a long time. While she was "dead" she said she could see her body below her, then she found herself in a real pretty meadow. (Which is weird, because I always thought that when I die I would first go to a pretty meadow — long before my Dad told me this story.) Then she saw a beautiful clear stream, and on the other side was Jesus holding out his arms to her. But the people she left on earth really wanted her back, and Jesus sent her back. She was revived and came back to her body.

He was very sick. The pneumonia was catching up with him. It was hard for him to breathe. It was about three in the morning. He was tired, but the pain kept him awake. Something came over him. It was calm and warm, like sleep. He let it take him over. The pain left. He couldn't hear his heartbeat or his breathing, but he didn't worry.

The morning came. It was beautiful, the best one he had ever seen.

The nurse came and looked at the writings on the machine above his headboard. Then she shut it off. She left the room, being sure she closed the door tightly and quietly.

He tried to talk, but his mouth was stiff and hard, as a matter of fact, his whole body was that way. He found that he could leave his body and float around the room. He couldn't see himself, only his body.

They took his body later that day. And as the urging inside told him to go up, up towards the sky — so he did.

At this point, discussion usually turned toward the possibility of reincarnation. If the kids were interested

enough, sometimes I brought in a friend, a psychic, who believes in reincarnation. As he shared his perceptions about the past lives of some of the students, there were some who felt he had touched a deep chord; these students were stimulated to explore what this belief might mean for them. He told one girl that he saw that she had been buried alive in a past life. She later told me that she had experienced an agonizing fear of enclosed spaces for as long as she could remember. Others saw the belief in reincarnation as misguided, or as outright quackery — and felt perfectly free to say so in their evaluations.

A part of my own education at this point had to do with letting go of my attachment to kids' belief systems. Like all of us, young people are in a sense on their own, trying to be autonomous and responsible human beings. They are growing, changing, learning. For many years to come, they will try on different attitudes and values. I found myself respecting and trusting them and realizing that they didn't *need* to be protected from belief systems different from their own.

One day when my psychic friend was talking about reincarnation, a mother was visiting the class. After the class, she told me she believed that a balancing perspective ought to be offered from the Christian point of view. I found it easy to feel the same respect for her that I felt for the students, and asked if she could suggest any speakers. When she realized that I genuinely wanted to cooperate in resolving her conflict about what the class was hearing, she arranged for an interesting young minister to address the class. He told the story, within a Christian context, of an older colleague, a dear friend, who had been clinically dead for an unusually long period. This person had had the experience of leaving his body, traveling rapidly toward a source of light, and being sent back to earth.

IF I DIE & WHEN I DO

As a result of this minister's talk, a mutual respect grew between the concerned mother and myself. We were both able to see that the kids did not jump onto a reincarnation bandwagon just because one persuasive speaker came along. This experience taught us both that young people are capable of making decisions for themselves, and that they will be making changes in themselves and their convictions all their lives.

At this point in the class, we frequently turned to a study of cultures for which a belief in reincarnation is integral — for example, the Buddhist and Hindu civilizations. As a result, the students expressed a refreshing range of creative concepts in their writing about life after death and reincarnation.

I believe very much in life after death. I think that people who die, their souls go into new bodies. I have a friend who occasionally has sharp pains in her back for no reason at all. Maybe in her past life she had a back injury, or had gotten stabbed in the back. I also know a little boy who probably has never heard of reincarnation. But sometimes he says things like, "I used to do that in my past life," or "I remember seeing that in my past life."

I don't think people who say they have been reincarnated are lying. Some people don't believe in this, but when they die they just may find out. When my day comes for me to die, it will be an exciting experience.

I believe in reincarnation because I have such a strong feeling that most of the things I do, I have done before.

WHO WAS I?

Was I rich, was I poor?
Was I exciting or a bore?

Did I dine at a Roman feast?
Was I a high Egyptian priest?

Did I cross the Delaware?
Not on the British side, I swear!

Whoever I was, whatever I'll be
I'll always try to be just me.

My Mom and Dad don't believe in reincarnation, and I don't know much about it so I can't say whether I believe in it or not. The fact that some people under hypnosis can speak foreign languages they have never learned is very hard to explain.

I think when I die, I'll come back as a different person. I had a dream about reincarnation.

I was killed in a car accident, and I was only 16. In school I was very popular, but when I died no one came to the funeral, not even my parents. It was as if I was a brat that wanted all the attention.

The only thing I remember was being put into a wall, but before they sealed me in, I got out and ran away.

I went straight to school. A new girl was there. She didn't look like me, but she acted like me. She ran around a lot like I used to. It was just as if there was someone else waiting to take my place after I died.

I don't believe in reincarnation. It just seems dumb to me because if you're stabbed with a knife there's no way it can heal up, and no scars be there and you come back to life again. It just seems phony to me. Even if I saw it with my own eyes, I would still just think it was a trick.

I don't believe in reincarnation because there's no way to prove it. If there is reincarnation, I don't think it's really me, because I can't remember anything from the life before. So what good is it? I would think I would be able to remember if the time is short from the time I died in my other life to the time I'm born again. But then again, I don't remember my birth. If I could do that, maybe I could remember my life before, if there was one.

I believe that after we die, our spirits stay with our friends and relatives for a few days, maybe, no longer. Then there's a meeting place (heaven?) where everyone goes and a head guy (God?) decides what, who, where we will be, go, next. Then we go through a factory-like process, and we are born another being.

Something kinda hit me today.
I looked at you and counted
All the times we had died.

THE OTHER LIFE

People were crying all around me. They kept saying things that would indicate that I was dead. But I wasn't!

I tried to say something, but realized I couldn't. I also tried to move. I couldn't do that either. The only sense that worked was hearing.

I don't know how long it was before they closed something over me. I guess it was my coffin.

When they lowered me into the ground, I knew it was the end. Everything went black.

The next thing I knew, I was staring into some doctor's face as he said, "Well, Mrs. Lahusick, you have a fine baby daughter." I was immediately taken away to be cared for by a nurse.

After a while, I saw the happy, flushed faces of fathers as they each searched for their own little child. I saw one of them staring at me, saying, "My girl, my own little girl."

"So, that's my father," I thought. He had a round, red face, short blond hair and brown eyes.

After a couple of hours, my parents started calling me some weird name like Wishanew.

My new life had started. As the nurse was carrying me through the hall, I noticed a calendar. At the top, it said May 2459.

"2459!!!" I thought, "Where did all the years go?" The only logical answer was that I had spent the time dead. At age 11 months I hadn't thought of anything better to explain it.

On my birthday something happened. I forgot everything about my other life. I didn't even remember I had had one.

IF I DIE & WHEN I DO

When I was ten, I started going to a psychiatrist like everyone else did. After I had been in hypnosis, my doctor told me I had talked about another life. I left his office wondering about it. My mother picked me up. As we pulled into the street another car screeched, and crashed into us.

The next thing I knew, people were crying all around me. They kept saying things that would indicate that I was dead. But I wasn't . . .

Young people are capable of great compassion and openness toward differing, deeply personal belief systems. They are full of questions and, by and large, are willing to review even those ideas that are most deeply rooted in them. Children do not simply adapt an older person's perspective. They ponder issues, discuss them with their peers, and constantly try to broaden their frame of reference. Religious and spiritual concerns have a compelling quality which attracts young and old alike.

After all our sharing of hopes and fears, of theories and dogmas, we still were faced by the ultimate mystery.

Death is . . .
a life beyond life that is a question.

Using Relaxation & Fantasy

9

*"The Me Inside Me
Is Somebody
Nobody Has Ever Seen"*

Picture a public school classroom. The floor is carpeted, with chairs and tables in a large rectangle facing the center of the room. The lights are out. There is a candle in the center with a few people around it. Students are sitting and lying in various places around the room, some on the floor, some under or on top of tables. It is totally silent, except for Erik Satie's music on the record player.

When the music ends, I quietly say, "Now allow your awareness to come to your body. Watch your breathing, move your fingers and toes a bit, and very gently come back to the classroom, feeling relaxed and calm and full of energy."

Bodies begin to move, a few sounds appear in the darkness as kids sit up. Some look at each other, others start talking about what has just happened, a few are still within themselves.

We automatically form a circle on the floor. Lights are turned on, the candle is blown out, class begins.

It is one thing to attempt to hold class when thirty

adolescents are tired, tense, full of sugar, bored, anxious, not there. It is quite another when they are relaxed, attentive, eager, and present. The remarkable changes that I perceived in my classroom due to the incorporation of relaxation exercises contributed profoundly to my own development. It was hard for me to grow when I found myself in an adversary or disciplinary role. The effects of several simple exercises encouraged me to shed more and more of my negative and stereotyped teacher roles.

Relaxation exercises helped kids let go of their defensive, fearful student roles. Primarily, these techniques served as a vehicle to reach deeper levels of experiences and feelings about death. Preparation for this exploration was important. It sometimes took experience with a number of different exercises before students felt that the process was of value.

Sometimes I feel embarrassed because some people feel that the whole thing of doing relaxation is dumb. I get into them, and people think I'm strange. If more people would try it, I would personally feel more comfortable.

The first time I did one, I didn't get into it because I felt like everyone was staring at me. The second time I really got into it. I hope we keep on doing them.

The first few times I felt sort of weird, but after a while I really started to like it. After I'm done relaxing, I feel sort of dizzy. My feet and hands get cold and my feet sort of fall asleep.

The exercises make me "uncomfortable." I wish I could explain what's wrong with me, but I can't. Maybe it's because I'm scared of my "feelings." Maybe some day I won't be so scared of them.

The exercises were really rewarding, they brought us all closer together. At first the experience was rather discouraging, at least for me. I simply imagined the images instead of them just coming into my head. This went on for several exercises. Then one time, it happened. My mind went blank, and while the record of the ocean played in the background, a boat suddenly floated across a murky, restless sea. The crew consisted of at least five sailors.

The fog began to roll in, and the fog horn began blaring. The boat seemed to belong to the year 1860 or earlier. I wasn't asleep, I was just barely aware of some sounds and activities. And I wasn't awake; I was between the two states.

At the close of the exercise, my foot jerked up violently. According to some theories, this would indicate an out-of-body experience. Also during the experience, a change occurred. At first, I was on the boat — not as part of the crew, but just on the boat. Then, I was above the boat and the crew, at the side. I was observing them, as they talked. I became aware of my surroundings just as the exercise was ending, as my foot jerked.

Many students found that the benefits and effects of the exercises extended beyond the boundaries of social studies classes, and even beyond school into their personal lives.

Ever since the first you taught it to us, I do it every night and it helps me to go to sleep. It makes me wonder why people don't use this instead of taking sleeping pills. Why don't more people know about this?

When we are doing the exercises, I find that I am not as nervous about tests as I used to be. They relieve tension and your muscles aren't so tight. I can also think a lot better, and in my last class it has taken a load off my shoulders.

In science we usually have a major exam once a month, and the exercises have made me relax a lot more about them. When I try to go to sleep, I get to sleep a lot faster and am not quite as tense as usual.

I was getting a low grade in the class that comes after this one. When I started relaxing, my grades started going up until all of a sudden I started getting "A's". Then when we stopped, my grades went down. Then we did it for a few days and I got a "B" on a test.

I think the exercises we do in class everyday really are helping me relax. In classes I get bored with, I find myself wandering off and I don't mind it at all. Also, when I'm really uptight about something, I can relax. And I'm always calm and never really nervous, now I know how to get relaxed any time I want to, and anywhere.

If I'm excited and nervous before a basketball game, I really try hard to do the exercises. This helps the "butterflies" to go away.

I really like doing the exercises, because by sixth period I'm usually all tensed up and rowdy. It calms me down, and helps me to not think about tests or fights that I've had during the day. And my arm (which was recently broken) is in pain at times during the day, and it helps me somehow forget the pain.

Would this be a good thing for people who are nervous? If so, the hospitals could get people more relaxed, so they wouldn't have nervous breakdowns.

There are today many sources with suggested exercises for relaxing and exploring inner space. *The Centering Book* (Gay Hendricks and Russell Wills, Prentice-Hall 1975) was the initial spark that inspired me to try out new ways of being with children. *The Second Centering Book* (Gay Hendricks and Tom Roberts, Prentice-Hall, 1977) was an additional aid.

We would begin each session with a basic relaxation or centering exercise. This involved having the students lie flat or sit straight, watch their breathing, and imagine each part of their bodies, starting with their toes, relaxing deeply.

At this point, I would frequently play some soft music or a record of the ocean or play my guitar and sing some songs.

We tried many variations on the core relaxation exercise. Some found it very easy to relax watching a candle. Others tried imagining a lighted stick floating over their bodies, relaxing each part. There were those who pictured themselves floating down, down, down, while others used upward motion as the way to let go of their tensions. The important thing was that each of them try different techniques (we often had several going at once) and be honest in reporting their experiences and their reactions.

> Sometimes I feel as if I am floating on a cloud of puffiness and air, as if someone is picking me up. . . . I really like the one where you put on the record of the heartbeat. It made me feel as if I were inside my mother's stomach.

> When we did the thing with the candle, everybody just faded out and the flame started celebrating to music.

> I like it better when there is music: it kind of blends out all the little interruptions and noises.

> A plant is a worryless thing. It doesn't have to worry if its dog dies. It wouldn't even know. In my exercises, I thought of a worryless plant, and someone on a floating raft.

> I was nowhere. It wasn't light but it wasn't dark. I wasn't here but I wasn't there.

I feel that I am lucky because I have been able to see some vivid pictures during these relaxation exercises. But I wonder why sometimes it is as though you are really there, and other times it is as though you are watching yourself. During one exercise I was in a meadow and I was laying in the deep grass and could look around me. Another time, when you put on some music, I was watching myself do a ballet.

I just saw laser illusions every time so far. . . . When you played the record of sounds I thought of an orchestra and bumblebees. When they were "singing" I got out of breath because they "sang" so long . . . the best time was when we were supposed to stop. I felt the most relaxed just then.

I felt I was in the middle of space, floating on a piece of clear jello. . . . I was on a big lazy Susan, which went any way I told it to.

I wasn't tired and I had a lot of energy. So I didn't think I could get into it. But surprisingly enough, I did. I wanted to think about playing tennis, because I love to play tennis. But in the background I kept seeing visions of my grandmother, because she just went into a nursing home today.

Today when you said, "Feel yourself sinking," it felt like I sunk all the way to Hawaii. I didn't see myself, I just saw other people swimming, surfing and shopping.

I didn't hear you at all. After a while of floating around in blackness, I started to fall and fall. Then I landed in the ocean. But I didn't drown. I could breathe normally and it was really neat.

When we did the "OM" exercise, I imagined myself standing on a mountain top overlooking a small village. I was wearing very tattered clothing and was dirty. Below in the village, strange-looking people were working. They were singing OM. They scared me quite a bit. It was cold and windy on the mountain, but sunny in the village. Then suddenly the whole picture was gone.

My dream started out for real in the class. You said to be in your favorite quiet spot, which happens to be my closet. My closet has shelves and clothes, white walls and a pewky green carpet. Then all of a sudden I was on a cliff, like one of the cliffs at Red Rocks. But it was in the middle of nowhere. All I could see was sky and big popcorn clouds. Then I found myself Hang-gliding (something I would really like to do). I could feel the wind blowing in my face and the sensation of being free. I felt as if I had never had a trouble in my whole life. Still all I could see was sky and clouds. My wonderful cliff had vanished. But I didn't care. All I cared about was being free. Your music was flowing all through my body. I was just flying around, past cities and towns and mountains. Then the music stopped. I started to fall, I mean straight down! Nose first! All I could see was my hang-glider disintegrating. Then big painted rocks! Talk about scary. I wish you wouldn't have turned off the music so fast.

I was very comfortable and relaxed. I like it when you play the guitar. I was laying by a stream with my hand in the water, and grass and flowers all around me.

When you said, "Pretend the candle flame is your balancing point," it got really warm in my stomach.

As soon as I began looking at the candle, I went into a trance. I began to sway — or so I thought — with the flame. I then felt I was the flame and began to get hot. Next I saw a figure in the flame and I went on seeing this figure the rest of the time until I came out of it. I saw that figure in my mind about 2½ months ago.

Today I feel relaxed and comfortable. When I came out of the exercise, Maura was snoring . . . When you played the "Om's" record, my body started to vibrate. First it was my arms, then my legs, then my stomach. I could also see a lot of OMs. The louder ones were bigger, and the quiet ones were smaller.

Today when we tensed our muscles I felt like the drawstring in a bag being tightened then being pulled apart when I let the tension out.

I was a tree today and the music was the wind blowing through me. It was warm. When Franki started to sing it was like rain.

When I'm doing the exercises, I remember things from my childhood that I never thought I could remember. I think of dreams I had when I was little. But when I try to remember dreams I've had for the last few days, I can't do it.

I was cross-country skiing and fell in a hole. Someone stuck a rope down and I started to climb it. When you told us to get up, I opened my eyes and my hands were climbing up the table leg like a rope. . . . I was in my closet, a grey rock rolled across my wall, over and over again. When the music started, the rock turned into a ballerina, and started dancing. . . . I was a piece of un-popped corn. All of the other pieces would start a conversation, and then they would leave. I thought it was unfair that they got to go and I didn't. . . .

There is a technique involved in conducting these exercises well. The students, via their blunt reporting of my errors, were my teachers.

You! I can't get over you, Franki! With these relaxation exercises you melt a person down like smooth and creamy butter, and all of a sudden out of a clear blue sky you open shades, turn on lights, "Get up, everybody!"

I imagined I was in a meadow with a big tree in the middle. When the music came on, the weeds started dancing and a whole bunch of field mice started playing instruments. The tree lifted me up so I could see better. I felt I was floating. When you started talking, Franki, it startled me and the tree dropped me. It made my back hurt.

I was "in it" really well this time: turn off the lights more often!

All I could do was remind them that I didn't know everything, that I made mistakes, that I was human. Sometimes the response came, "But you're the teacher!" Once I turned to the blackboard, and started hitting my head against the wall while repeating, "Teachers don't know everything! Teachers don't know everything!" Eventually students realized that they were co-creators in what took place in the classroom.

I found that before young people were able to experience and acknowledge their deepest fears and concerns about death, there had to be a willingness to go inside, an appreciation of being alone with themselves.

On one of my classroom walls there was a poster that said,

BEING ALONE IS BEING WITH SOMEONE.

I believe that coming to realize the truth of this statement was one of the most positive results of the relaxation exercises. Some young people discovered, for the first time, that they really were not alone — for they had themselves, and they themselves were good friends to be with. At this age, the desire to be always in the company of others can become a compulsive need not to be alone. I watched this attitude undergo change.

IF I DIE & WHEN I DO

I think the relaxation thing gives you a good idea on what you really are inside. It lets you get into yourself, and gives you a chance to relax, calm down, and let your mind wander. You become what you really are deep down.

The me inside me is someone nobody has ever seen. During the relaxation exercises I can be that somebody nobody ever sees. I can do the things I don't usually get to do. It doesn't matter where I am. When I am by myself, I am not afraid, because I know that nothing can hurt me. There is no tension and nothing to worry about. All I have to do is to let myself go.

During the exercises I always walk through these mirrors. I usually get a cold feeling inside me. The mirrors are very shiny, they bounce off of everything. They practically blind me because they reflect on everything that's close to them. But it's a quiet place to go when I'm feeling down-right blue. The reason why I go there is because some-times I get afraid of people so I go there where it's nice and quiet.

A lot of times I can get inside my body and see myself there as a little tiny person walking around and relaxing myself completely.

I like relaxation, because it lets me be what I want, do what I want. When you're in your own little world, no-one can tell you you're acting dumb.

*After this class is over, I am going to keep doing relax-
ations, and keep writing down my experiences.*

*During relaxation, when I go inside myself, I find just
colors and curved lines. No bones, blood and guts but
just warmth. The colors and warmth are all in the lower
back and as I relax they expand, crawling, reaching out,
growing into new things, new worlds. Sometimes I hear
music (I think my life is based on music) to where I can
hear each note on each instrument. Personally I would
like to have these exercises each day.*

*As the sun turns the sky aglow with color,
I feel peace coming across me,
The same way I feel when
I'm alone in the mountains
On a cool, dark forest path,
At ease with myself, and the
World around me*

Not only were students less afraid of being alone, they
also discovered entire realms within themselves that gave
them cause to reflect that they were more than they knew.
One of our favorite experiences was taken from *Mind
Games* by Jean Houston and Robert Masters. The exercise
involves going into a closet and seeing a door in the back of
the closet. The journey takes the explorer down a stone
staircase to a black pool of water, and into a boat that
floats downstream and out into beautiful sunshine and
green meadowland. I usually ended this exercise with the
theme from Mozart's Piano Concerto in C (the "Elvira
Madigan" theme). There was a great sense of peace in the
room.

My Unicorn

A lot of times when we do relaxation exercises I see a unicorn. I'm usually riding him or standing beside him. He's pure white and has a golden horn. Ever since I was little I've always wanted to have a unicorn.

145

Sometimes I would ask the students to go to their favorite place and be whoever they wanted to be and do whatever they wanted to do. At this point, while some people were all over the universe, others were still sitting quietly in their closet. They were all opening up to their inner selves and beginning to sense their own magnificence.

In my world there is a door, on the door there is a tiny golden knob that opens my door into a world all my own. In my world there are millions of other worlds, most of which are unexplained. The knob will only turn if my world wants to let me in. There are happy, scary, beautiful and wonderful things in my world. There are endless places to go, things to see and feelings to feel in my world. My world can be a wonderful or a horrible place to go.

We live behind a fence
with no desire to create a gate
that will allow us to be free.
There are no limits behind or ahead
but we're too lazy and scared
to do anything about it.

Imagination is a door
so simple to open,
but we're frightened
of what's behind it.

We're not limited,
but we build our own fence
around ourselves.
It's not friends, parents
or neighbors — it's you, you
build your own fence
of limits.

Relaxation exercises provided us with, among other things, the opportunity to be with ourselves, to let out some of our tension, to discover new parts of ourselves, and to experience other dimensions in which we could work and play.

The door to my
room is shut.
But I am not shut
in.
I am alone
but I am not lonely.
My mind is enclosed
in my body.
Yet it is free to
wander,
I am content to sit
alone and ponder,
In my dreams I am
a thousand people.
And all of them
are what I am
totally at ease
knowing that no
one
can take me away
from myself,
I am free.

When students were relaxed I had them explore, in that state, a certain aspect of death. To relive a death experience, I asked them to do some of the following:

Allow whatever comes into your mind. Watch it, then let it go.

Now, allow memories of your first experience with death to come in.

This could have been when you first heard of death.

This could have been the death of a pet.

This could have been the death of a person.

Be inside yourself. Allow images to come. Allow feelings to come. Watch them.

How did you first hear about death?

Did someone tell you?

How did you respond? Did you have questions?

What did you do?

Did someone stay with you, or were you alone?

Do you recall any sights, sounds, smells, or tastes connected with this death?

What part of your body reacted most to this experience?

How did other people around you react to this death?

Here is what some of the students wrote:

I was 7 or 8 when my turtle died. My mother and father were with me. My father had a gold shirt and blue pants on, my mother had a red shirt with white polka dots and blue pants. My father was lying on the ground. I felt horrible because my little sister was the one who killed my turtle.

I had an awful picture in my mind. Last summer our dog ran into the street and got hit by a car. My Mom brought him into the garage and said I should wait with him while she called the doctor. I saw the picture of what really happened, and my dog was lying on my pants. My mind kept picturing the blood that he bled on me. When you said to just let it melt away, my body felt awful tense.

It was black all around, with sad faces, long, long, sad faces. Everyone crying. Me thinking that I had just seen him that morning. I wouldn't believe it. He was my friend. I was only five. When you asked us to remember, that's what I remembered. But I usually don't like to think of that stuff.

I saw my Dad crying, sitting on a green couch. I felt hot and black inside. I saw my Dad very clearly, but no-one else did. I went over and hugged him. I was six years old.

When I was at the funeral I kneeled down by my grandfather's casket. I put my hand under the blanket thinking that my grandfather would hold my hand. I was only seven, and I didn't understand what was going on. The room was full of flowers, and people crying. I just saw myself sitting on the sofa with my cousins.

I went back to the time my grandmother died. The room she was in seemed dark and musty, as if millions of dead bodies had been there before. Or as if some devil-like

Using Relaxation & Fantasy

person was looking down on me and laughing, "Ha, ha! You could be next, you know!"

Then the people around were gone, and I was there all alone. It was all silent. My grandmother was white as a sheet. Just before I got up, all of a sudden there was a bright light in my eyes.

Yesterday, in the exercise, I could see the pallbearers and smell the flowers and the perfume of the dead man's wife. I could see everyone's face clearly.

When I came home from school one day, my Mother told me my pet bird had got out of the cage. It flew into the windows several times and then died. We buried it out in the back yard. In the exercise, I remembered seeing the brown of the dirt and the green of the grass and leaves. I remembered the feeling that I wanted my bird back, and that somehow I would get it back. But I knew inside that I wouldn't.

I was watching the light, and everything went black. Then I saw my Grandpa who has been dead for five years and I started to cry when he tried to talk to me. I wanted to touch him, but I couldn't, so I just kept crying.

Jeffrey Schrank's book, *Teaching Human Beings: 101 Subversive Activities for the Classroom* (Boston: Beacon Press, 1972), has a chapter entitled "Learning About

Death." One of the suggestions in this chapter is to have students experience their own funeral. When my class did this exercise, the results were remarkable. Once the students were relaxed, I began:

You have died.

You are in a funeral parlor, and people are coming to see you.

What are the sights, the sounds, the smells?

Who is there?

How are they acting?

How are they feeling?

What are they saying?

What would you like to say to some of the people?

How are you feeling?

What is the service like?

Here are some responses:

I laid down on my back, with my palms up. I was fairly tense. You told us we had just died, and were in our casket at the funeral. I was rather surprised you would tell us that, but I did what you said.

Soon I was lying in a casket with the lid closed, but over my face was a piece of glass so you could look in. I could see the color black all around me. My family and a few friends were there. (That's the kind of funeral I would prefer.) They were all wearing black and crying. No-one

*was laughing. (Thank goodness!) I could smell gloomi-
ness and, strangely enough, dust. I also heard my favorite
songs playing.*

*I saw my Mom with my 8-month-old sister in her arms.
She was saying that she wanted me to come back to her
and that my sister would miss me. I wanted to tell her that
everything was OK, but she couldn't hear me and just
kept crying. Then my Aunt came and took her away. My
mind said that I was dead but I knew I was still alive.*

*My funeral parlor was pink and was very small and
smelled bad. I saw my Mom crying above the casket. I
didn't feel like jumping out and saying, "I'm O.K." I just
felt like crying also.*

*Today when I was in my coffin, there were roses all
around me. I could smell them. At my funeral were a lot
of people I didn't know. I think they were people I met in
high school, college, work. My Mother was leaning over
me and crying. I couldn't see if my Dad was crying, but he
was trying to calm my Mother. Then I saw my sister. She
was smiling. I don't know why, I guess because she is
mad with me today. I think she loves me. (Well, I hope
she does.)*

*Then the minister was saying what a good childhood I
had, went to good schools and my parents really loved
and cared for me. That I had a good home, lots of friends
and things like that. Then they closed the lid on the coffin
and carried me out and put me in a big hole and put dirt
over me. Then they played some music. After the music
stopped, the guy started talking again. They threw flowers*

IF I DIE & WHEN I DO

on me. All I could really be sure about was the smile on my sister's face.

Every once in a while, my Mom would come by and cry on my grave. I couldn't see everything that was engraved on my headstone, but I think it said "Born 1964, Died 2001. Lived in California with her Mother."

I saw myself at a wake. There were lots of flowers and people. The funeral home was dark and dingy. People were looking down at me and crying and saying how real I looked. Then I saw myself and the inside of my coffin. I had on an ugly pink print dress. The inside of my coffin was pink velvet. I hate pink! It absolutely makes me sick.

By this time I was really getting mad. I decided to look outside. It was a gorgeous, beautiful, sunny summer day. If they were going to do this, they could at least hold it outside! My gorgeous day was interrupted by the fighting of my Mother and Grandmother. "She needs pink," my Grandmother was saying, "She's a girl. A big funeral is a family tradition." Then my Mom said, "But this is not at all what she wanted. She wanted to be cremated and have a small funeral."

If I could have talked, I would have said, "You two are absolutely amazing. Yes, Mom, I wanted a cremation and a small funeral. I want a different dress on right now. And I want to be taken outside! And this whole experience would have been more pleasant if you two wouldn't have fought."

I hope to God this doesn't happen. If it does, I'll be really upset.

There were some students who, along with their parents, thought that discussions about death constituted religious education. Although I communicated my feelings about the exercises and hoped everyone would experience them, I allowed individual students to decide whether or not they would participate.

It was not my place to force kids to deal with any issue, especially one as personal as death. It was my place to offer the opportunity. It is true that when the doors are opened and young people begin exploring their inner worlds, there can be fearful, dark, or angry experiences. There can also be joyful experiences. Each of us has our own timing in confronting these aspects of ourselves. Some students decided to deal with their inner experiences. Others chose to postpone this process. I simply respected their individual decisions.

But I felt free to share my belief that when we bring our negative feelings into our conscious minds and experience them fully, their hold on our lives is over. I was not, at the time of teaching these courses, a trained psychologist; when situations with individual students arose that went beyond my realm of competence, I did not hesitate to call in a counselor, a psychologist, or a social worker from the school.

However, I found that for most of the students the relaxation exercises and the subsequent explorations of inner feelings about death led to an increased understanding of self and a healthier attitude about death and life.

> When I'm in relaxation I feel an immense sense of tranquility. I can be, or do anything I want. When I come out of relaxation, I feel a certain understanding of myself. I feel closer to the real me, inside and outside.

Death
in Dreams
& Nightmares

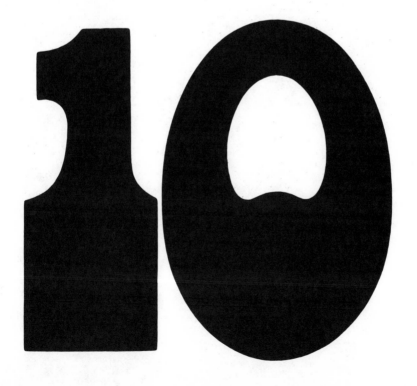

"When They Put Me Down in the Ground,
My Parents and Sisters Threw Weeds"

From scientific research on sleep, we now know that we all dream more than a thousand dreams each year. Yet most of us have lost touch with the meaning of our dreams. We may think we hardly ever dream, and that even if we do, our dreams have no significance. Consider the following incident reported by a student while we were studying the world of dreams.

> *My Dad had a dream last night. All of a sudden he started to scream. He felt like he was split in half. Half of him was in the air and couldn't scream. The other half was on the land and screaming bloody murder. Everything else was totally blanked out. He woke up petrified. My Mom noticed that he was white, shaking and almost crying. He refused to go back to sleep for fear it would happen again.*

As with most people in our culture, this man's attitude upon awakening showed that he viewed his dream not as a communication, but as something quite separate and inexplicable. Had he been aware of the possibilities of communications from himself contained in the dream, his reaction might have been different. He might have been grateful for the message, and taken this as a positive incentive to make changes in his life.

There is something extraordinary about our cultural rejection of dreams, considering that an important method of healing those who break down psychologically is to help them get themselves together by learning to understand the meaning of their own dreams. If we want to promote mental health, instead of waiting until it is necessary to cure breakdowns, we could try helping our children to learn something about the messages their dreams are bearing.

When the twisting sun brushes the moon, and the multi-colored sticks of beauty spear the shimmering stars. When thin folds of cool, white air drift through sharpened spears of silver tin, and a clear running mist of deep, blue liquid forms rolling waves as it dips around a crooked tree trunk, then, you know you are dreaming.

Lying in bed at night
Fighting that monster with all your might
Flying up in the sky
Watching the years go by
Dream what you want
Let the beasts haunt
Be a movie star or singer
Let the memories linger

Once upon a sleep
I heard a loud Beep! Beep!
So I ran to the window
And saw a pink jeep.
I put in my hair
A lovely blue bow
Then I hopped down the stairs
Chased by ten bears
Then I leaped to the jeep
And drove down the street
With the heat at my feet!

Dreams are funny
They are almost real
Yet everything seems
To float away.

Dreams are wonderful
In them you can do
Anything.

Some dreams are brilliant
Some are faint
When you get to the good part
Someone wakes you up,
And the dream is gone.

BE YOUR DREAM

I like to dream,
because it gives me a chance to try to understand myself.

In my dreams
I see myself in different ways and places.
I see myself in meadows, lakes and mountains,
and faraway places I used to know.
I dream of old friends and new friends,
and people I've never met, who are familiar to me.
And sometimes my dreams are about me and me alone.

It was during our exploration of death-related fears that many students began writing about fearful dreams and nightmares.

I had a dream that I was the last person on earth. Whenever I would look at something, it would disappear. Then one day, I looked in the mirror, and I disappeared too.

When I was six I had a nightmare that my Mom was run over by a giant penny. It was controlled by a man dressed all in black, who looked like Sherlock Holmes. My Mom was walking down the street when the huge shiny copper penny came rolling towards her. It hit her, and there she was lying on the street, dead.

I was at our farm and had walked out to the barn to see my horse. When I came back to the house, I couldn't find anybody. I learned to manage by myself. Every night, at the same time, someone walked by the house but never came close. One night, I ran out to him. He turned towards me and he had my face! He started to choke me, and I woke up.

Some of the worst hallucinations happen when I'm sick. One of them starts off with me lying in bed. I look up and notice the roof is made from toothpicks. I look at my fingers and watch them grow and twine all around the room, then up toward the roof. I know that if they touch the roof, all of the toothpicks will fall and stab me. My fingers start to grow faster and faster. Just as they are about to hit the roof, I scream and fall unconscious.

I had a dream that I died in my sleep. I was buried in a six-foot, see-through casket, standing up. A man came and took me out of the casket and led me to a stream of green silky water. He said that if I could jump over it without falling into it, he would let me go back to living again. But when I tried I fell in. My whole body was solid green, and all I could see around me was green sparkly stuff. The man said I could go back to my house just to visit, but when I got there my whole family was out at a party. I went looking around the house to see if anything had changed, but nothing had. Then the man appeared and told me I had to go back with him. I started crying green tears. He told me that the longer I cried, the longer I would stay dead.

I was invited to a party at a girl's house, which sat on top of a hill above a graveyard. All around was an old dried-up hedge, which climbed up the walls like millions of snakes. As I opened the door, it creaked with a ghostly sound, and an eerie feeling came over me. I heard the clicking of heels on the cold marble floor. Looking up the hall, I saw a girl walking towards me. She had a weird little smile on her face, and as she came closer, I saw she had a dagger in her hand. She started walking faster, then she raised the dagger and I saw the cold blackness in her eyes.

IF I DIE & WHEN I DO

I turned and ran down the large corridor to the foot of the stairs, and found that I was standing in a puddle of blood. I heard the girl coming and started up the stairway. The horrible laugh behind me made me quicken my pace.

At the top of the stairs I came to a door. I put my hand on the door knob. It was as cold as ice. I could hear my heart beating as if it were in my ears. I took a deep breath and flung the door open. A vacuum-like wind sucked me through the door and hurled me into darkness. I was spinning, and all around me I could hear people screaming. But above all, I could hear the horrid laughter of the girl behind me. It was as if I was falling endlessly, helplessly into space. I could see the bottom of the pit coming toward me. I screamed. All of a sudden there was a terrible pain, then everything went dark.

Ann Faraday, in *The Dream Game* (New York: Harper & Row, 1974), remarks that there is a longstanding belief that dreams about dying can actually foreshadow impending death. If this were really true, she says, the world would long since have been depopulated! Most people who work with dream symbolism agree that death is a metaphor.

If the feeling in the following poem had come through a dream it would have been expressed by a death.

A DEATH WITHIN ME

This isn't really a death,
But a long-lost friend.
Tracee, she moved last summer.
We were really close to each other,
But now she's gone,
She's moved away.
But, it's a sort of death.
I told her this once in a letter.
She wrote back to me,
"Kathy, you always said
Everyone has to go,
But you are close to me
No matter how far apart we are."
And she was right. There are
Always memories. She won't be gone
Forever. I'll see her again.
Still, it's a small death.

We use death metaphorically many times in our daily language. "If looks could kill, she would have been dead." "When you say things like that, you kill me." "If I had to do that, I'd be scared to death." "While I was waiting to go on the stage, I died a thousand times." "I'd rather die than go through that again." "When my Mom came into the room and saw me, I could have died."

Around the time that my parents were going through a divorce, I had many dreams that my Mom died, and my Dad would never care.

Many unacknowledged perceptions and feelings about family relationships come to children through dreams. It is sad that, in the normal course of their lives, they rarely have anyone to help them discover what these dreams are trying to say to them — no way to "get the message" that might help them deal better with difficult situations. All they can do is to look sadly at the simple story lines of the dreams, which tell that brothers want to kill them, sisters laugh over their graves, and parents want them out of the way.

I had a nightmare that was so frightening that, ever since, it has been one of my biggest fears. Soon after midnight, my Mom and Dad woke me up, got me dressed and took me to the car. I said, "Where are you taking me?" They said, "To get an ice cream cone." They took me to a place I had never been before. My Mom gave me three cents, which isn't enough to buy an ice cream cone. Not only that, but they are not open that late at night. But I walked in front of the car towards a brick wall. All of a sudden, my Dad turned on the lights, started up the car, and ran over me, smashing me up against the wall. And they were so piggy, my Mom got out and ran to me and took the three cents out of my hand.

My brothers were trying to kill me. I was on the counter in my kitchen, and my brothers put snakes all around me. They could jump high, so I had to jump really high and run fast. I had this dream a lot of times.

We were driving up a skinny mountain road. When we got to the top, Dad parked the car at the edge of the mountain. I was afraid of falling. I opened the door and got out, but there was no ground. I screamed for my mother and father as I fell down, down, down. I saw them at the edge of the mountain. They were just waving to me. "Goodbye," they called. I saw the rocks below. My eyes popped open.

In my dream someone rang the doorbell and I answered it. It was a murderer. He said, "I came to kill you." My Mom said, "Wait, she has to clean her room first. Then you can kill her." She gave me a broom.

I had a dream that my Mom had to kill everyone in our family, but first she had to cut off all of our fingers with a paper cutter. After she cut off our fingers, she gave us some medicine that made us all about one inch tall.

My family found an old shack, and moved in. I hated living there. I was helping my Mom cook, and my Dad was outside with my brothers. I kept hearing a lion roaring. I went outside and asked my Dad what had happened to my brothers. He gave me this weird, scary smile, and said he fed them to the lion. He started coming toward me.

In my dream I was in a castle. My Dad was the King and my Mother was the Queen. My Mom gave me some rollerskates that made me fly and said, "Get out of here before the King kills you." I flew away. He shot me in the arm. I said, "Stop it." He hit me again, in the body, and I fell from the sky.

We were on the road. I asked Mom where we were going. "I don't know," I heard her murmur. "Can you stop so I can get an ice cream?" "No," she replied harshly. "Wanta play cards, Dad?" No answer. "Mom, is Dad in a bad mood?" "No, he's dead. I killed him." "Why, Mom, why? Did you get in a fight? WHAT HAPPENED?" The next thing I knew, she was after me. "Please Mom, no!" But it happened. I was dead.

We were going downtown at night and it was dark and rainy. My Dad stopped the car in the middle of the street and locked the doors. He lit a match and tried to set the car on fire. I screamed and yelled. My sister was out there looking at me and Dad, but she didn't know what to do. I got out of the car and ran to her, crying. Now I often look at my Dad, and say to myself, "He wouldn't do a thing like that to me or anyone else!"

My big sister and I shared a room and we were always fighting. My dream, that I had over and over, started with my sister and I going down our dusty basement stairs. We would sit on the bottom stair, fighting over a doll. It was a pretty one, with an old-fashioned smock dress, two black crosses for eyes, a button for a nose and a mouth made out of red velvet. After the fighting had gone on for a while, my sister would throw the doll at me and run up *the stairs as fast as she could. She would lock the door behind her, and I would bang on it. But I couldn't get out. Then the doll would blow up like a bomb and blow me up, too.*

Our family had a boat and invited some friends to go with us water-skiing. We all took turns, and when mine came my brother said, "While you're skiing, will you look under the water?" So I said I would. The boat was leaking oil, and after looking under it, I stood up and I couldn't see. I was blind and my family didn't care!

I heard a noise. When I turned around, there was a man with a knife. He stabbed me. I was lying in a coffin, with a blue satin lining. My mother and my father were crying over my body and my sisters were laughing. When they put me down in the ground, my parents and my sisters threw weeds.

In more than half the nightmares recorded by my students, they woke up just before the dreaded event happened. "I opened my mouth to yell for help, but no sound would come. Just when I knew I was going to die, I woke up." "They took out a giant knife, and it went straight at my neck with a full swing. I suddenly woke up before it hit me." The students were intrigued when we studied a different culture, where from an early age children are taught to face up to danger and fear in dreams, and to fight back.

The children of the Senoi, a tribe in Malaya, are encouraged to take their dreams seriously as an important part of their lives. They are educated to confront hostile forces in dreams and to fight them. If the menacing image fights back, they are to call on friendly powers to assist them, and to battle if necessary to the death. There is a long history of traditional beliefs behind this manner of dealing with dreams. The tribe believes that bad dreams are an indication of warring energies (hostile spirits) within the dreamer's inner self. If these are not dealt with, they will become alienated from his larger self, and will divide him against himself and his fellows. The tribal wisdom asserts that the threatening image, after it has been defeated in the dream, turns into a friendly helper. Thus, the psychic energy that would otherwise have remained bound up in the conflict is released for cooperative and joyful living. It is significant that the interest in Senoi dream psychology was generated by an early observer's curiosity as to how this particular tribe managed to be so democratic, nonviolent, cooperative, and self-sufficient, and to live in such apparent harmony with natural forces and with each other.

Here is what one student wrote about the Senois:

Senoi dreamers,
What are they about?
They are a nice little tribe
Without any doubt.

They try to conquer nightmares
And remember their good dreams,
And they always do it,
At least that's how it seems.

They hardly have any
Crimes in their city,
That's better than ours,
For ours ain't too pretty!

They're so peaceful a tribe
It's hard to believe!
But I'm happy where I live
And I wouldn't leave.

The amount of time we were able to spend on dreams, only one element in a brief course, was severely limited. Even so, some students started working with the Senoi technique and were strengthened by the results. One boy was beset by an ugly Fat Lady in his dreams and fantasies. He described several encounters with her to the class:

> I was on a mountain base and a stream was nearby. The Fat Lady appeared and took my pack. I pulled it away from her and pushed her in the stream, which flowed to the ocean. I was tired so I took my canoe, floated down the stream and took a nap on the beach. And she came and took my pack and canoe. I ran after her and then from her. I saw sharks swimming, so I picked her up and threw her in the water. The sharks started to nibble.

But she was not to be defeated so easily.

> In the relaxation exercise with the candle, I drifted off and soon I was looking at the candle with nobody in the room except me. That Fat Lady came in and blew out the candle. I threw her through the wall, and she came back in. I carried her out of the social studies area, which had become a boat, and threw her into the water.

There were several more encounters of a similarly strenuous kind. The student became almost philosophical about his adversary.

And indeed, after a few more battles, the Fat Lady stopped pestering him.

As we discussed what is known about dreams, many kids became fascinated observers of their own dreaming processes. They noted that sometimes they "woke up" in

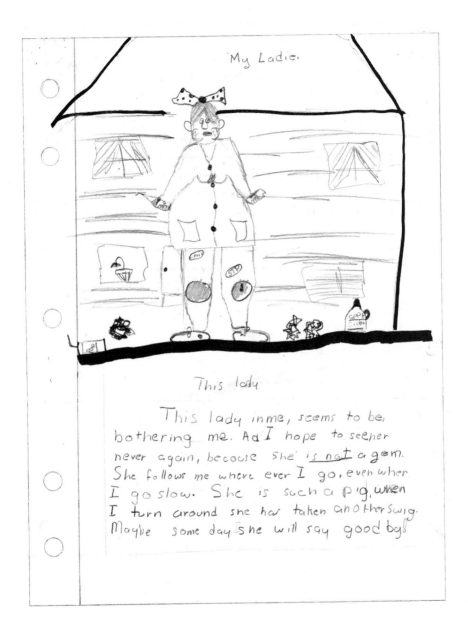

My Ladie

This lady

This lady in me, seems to be,
bothering me. Aa I hope to see her
never again, becouse she is not a gem.
She follows me where ever I go, even wher
I go slow. She is such a pig, when
I turn around she has taken another swig.
Maybe some day she will say good by!

dreams, only to find out later that it was another stage of dreaming. They became aware of the different roles they played in their dreams: sometimes seeming to be a participant, sometimes an unseen observer, sometimes changing from one role to another within the same dream. They became sensitive to the colors and landscapes and sounds of their dreams.

The most significant death in a dream is our own. It can symbolize the death of an outgrown part of ourselves. From this can come the birth of expanded and more inclusive parts of ourselves.

We may one day decide that dreams are an important part of life, and that interpreting their messages to us is a vital part of knowing ourselves. Then, perhaps, we shall find out more about the dreams of adolescents, and how to help them to make use of this extraordinary interior theater to develop themselves in a kindly and self-accepting way.

Death is like a dream —
You live with it,
You realize it,
You experience it.
There's no getting out of it.
It comes by itself.

Opening Up
to the
Paranormal

I Felt As If I Were Outside,
Watching My Own Accident

One day I was reading aloud from a book that explored Tibetan practices and beliefs about death. I came to a passage about a Buddhist monk who spent his entire life in a small hut on a Himalayan mountainside. He supposedly traveled outside of his body much of his life. As I read this, I looked around the room. Several kids were looking surprised — as though a light bulb had just gone on.

"Have any of you experienced leaving your body?"

A few raised their hands. This began an ongoing, involving discussion of "weird" and inexplicable events experienced by the students. They disclosed, most for the first time, happenings that they had thought indicated craziness or stupidity.

My commitment was to an atmosphere of freedom, acceptance, and humor. Given the level of my own growth at the time and the situation in which I was teaching, I perceived my role to be one of allowing and encouraging recognition of "unusual" experiences. It was a conscious decision to continue inviting such discussions. And I did have many students come to me as a sympathetic listener for such experiences.

177

In many areas of psychology, and certainly in death education, it is a basic tenet that the denial of one's experiences and emotions can lead to neurotic patterns and distorted living. Therefore, I consistently reminded students that they could have experiences which were valid even if hard to understand.

Among other experiences, students spoke of visions, dreams that seemed to them profoundly significant, out-of-body travel, premonitions of events that subsequently came true.

When we open our perceptions to include such experiences, it profoundly affects our view of what is real, what is possible, and what kind of beings we are. This, in turn, changes our view of what it means to be alive and what is the significance of death.

When I was in a car accident, I was knocked unconscious for about five seconds. I felt as if I were outside, watching my own accident. It was a warm feeling. All I could see were people and the accident; everything else was silver-white. Then I came conscious. The reason why I never said anything about this before was that I thought people would think I was dumb.

My friend and I were talking about who we would cry for more if they got killed, and I decided I would cry more for my dog. You know I love my parents very much, but my dog was something very special to me. We were walking across the fields to get something to eat, and my dog was off the leash. All of a sudden we heard a smash and a howl. When we got there, my dog was lying in the street dying. The strange thing is that in some way, I knew it was going to happen.

This happened to a good friend of mine recently. After she had been asleep for a while, she felt something cold scratching her leg. She woke up, and there was a spiral notebook lying beside her. She had never seen it before, so she picked it up to see what was in it. Inside it said that someone close to her was going to die in a car wreck very soon. She laid the notebook down and went to sleep. In the morning, her Mom told her that her favorite uncle had died in a car accident that night. She showed her Mom the notebook, and her Mom had never seen it before either. The weird thing was that it was her own handwriting in the book.

Last year I bought a beautiful fantail goldfish and named it Princess. I thought it might get lonesome so I also bought two plain goldfish. One night I woke up and had to go to the bathroom. I went into the room where my goldfish were kept and for some reason I was very scared. I walked over to the fish bowl and Princess was lying on the pink rocks. Instead of gold her body was white, even her eyes, and the other two fish were eating her. I ran to my room and cried myself to sleep. Ever since then, I've wondered why, when I hardly ever wake up at night, I'd pick that night of all nights to wake up?

We were at our condominium. We had just got out of school for Christmas and I got new skis. That night I dreamed I would break my leg. It was like a nightmare. The next day I got up early to go to the slopes. Me and my brother took a hard slope. It was the first run of the season. We got down half the slope and I didn't fall once. Then I just kind of plopped over and broke my leg.

One day, my mother and I were driving down the road. We came to an intersection and had to stop because a funeral was going by. For no reason, my mother started talking about her friend M. When the funeral passed, we started the car and went home. When we got there my father told us that M. had died in a car accident that day.

My uncle couldn't sleep the night after my grandmother died. He sat up on his couch and was smoking a cigarette when he looked up and saw a white, misty figure of a woman. While that happened, and he was thinking about life after death and whether Grandma would live any longer, the figure changed into some kind of a symbol. He put his cigarette out to see if the smoke was doing it, *but it wasn't. It stayed there for about 15 minutes. The next week he opened a book, and there it was, the exact same symbol he had seen a week before! Underneath the symbol, it said, "INFINITE." I think, and so does my uncle, that my Grandma was trying to tell him that there is life after death.*

One night I slept over at a friend's house and that night we both dreamed the same dream! In the morning I was halfway telling her what I had dreamed when she started to tell me the second half. It turned out to be the same as mine.

When I was about seven, I was with a younger friend. I joked around with him, and told him that a creek bed nearby was filled with dollar bills. We walked down to the creek. Some older kids were there. They dug up some sand, and there was a dollar bill.

One time when I was about 7 years old, I had a dream of my great-grandmother falling and falling. She was hurt badly. The next week we heard that she was in the hospital because she fell down the stairs and broke her hip. (And I was in Colorado and she was in Chicago.)

When I was about six years old my sister and I shared a bunk bed. Since I was older, I slept on top. I usually slept with a stuffed tiger. One night I got this strange feeling that my blankets were being lifted off me, and something took the tiger out of my arms. Suddenly, but gently, I floated up, and then down to the ground behind our hassock. The whole room was softly lighted by an unknown light. I could see the door to the hall across the room. It was very dark there. All the time there was this noise like a group of people talking at once, but their voices were muffled. Then, very clear and sharp, I could hear something rustling out in the hall, slowly. I knew it was something coming to get me, so I tried to scream for my mother, but no sound came out. Then all the noise stopped and I quickly floated back into bed, and everything was put back.

Is it a monster?
What can it be?
Is it living?
I can't see.

Is there only one?
Two, maybe three?
Skinny or big?
I can't see.

I wish you still were here
then it could be "we."
Is the thing still here?
I can't see.

This darkness —
Is it me?
Lord, lend me your eyes
So that I might see.

My Mom once dreamed that her Dad was telling her that her Mom had been hurt, but he wouldn't tell her if she was dead. My Mom got so upset that she called her mother, who lives in Indiana, to see if she was alright. Her mother said she had fallen down the stairs and hurt herself. She said she couldn't get to sleep and was thinking about my Mom all night because she was in so much pain.

Thursday morning, first period, I saw my teacher's "aura." It was a kind of bluish-green color. I wasn't trying to see it, it just happened. I only saw it around her head.

It all started on a dark December night. I was jogging with my dog and this dark fog was standing in front of me. I touched it, and I couldn't get my hand out. My dog saw me struggling so he started biting the fog. I finally got my hand out, and it was all raw and red. I saw my dog disappearing into the fog. I grabbed his tail and pulled and finally it came off.

The next morning, I told my Mom about my nightmare. She said something like it had really happened. My dog had been trying to catch a cat and ran under a tractor. My Mom tried to pull him out and his tail came off in her hand.

Ever since I was about six years old I always thought that there were little mice playing banjos under my bed. If I had to go to the bathroom or something I would always *be afraid because I thought they would come out and get me. I knew, and I was almost positive, that they were real because I could hear the banjos playing. But if I ever looked under there at night, I would die. So I never could see them. But I could still hear the banjos playing. When I woke up in the morning I would look under my bed as best I could, but they were not there, because you could only see them at night. Sometimes it still happens to me.*

This dream that I had bothered me because it was a true dream. I dreamed that my grandfather died, and I kept on having dreams about him. Then I stopped having them and forgot about them. But a week or so later, he did die and we went to his funeral.

One night I was lying in bed thinking about my Uncle who had cancer and was very sick. When I fell asleep I had a dream that my parents were called to the hospital. When they finally got there they found out he had just died. I woke up crying because I really thought he had died, but my Mom told me it was just a dream. The next day when I got home from school my Mom looked very sad. She told me that my Uncle had died about an hour ago. I was sad and scared because I had just had that dream last night.

We bring our kids with athletic gifts to a high pitch by providing them with coaches and expensive physical facilities. I am intrigued by contemplating what kinds of wise superstars might develop if we were to educate spiritual and psychic talents.

I had, every year, a few students who consistently displayed striking psychic qualities. Some flavor of the nature of their gifts and of the essence of their being may cling to the following stories.

I was raised in a family where the big joke was on ESP. But it's still hard to convince me that communication and information is always obtained in the usual way. I can sometimes, in dreams and by looking at people and other things, pick up a very important part of what someone will say or do sometime soon. I hardly ever tell people I do this, because I'm still working on convincing myself I can actually predict things and tune in on things, and be able to prove my predictions to myself as correct. I like to try to feel what people are feeling so I can help in whatever way is best. It's hard to explain what I do that lets me see these things, but I'll try.

I close my eyes and instantly focus on a cloudlike atmosphere where an image will come into the clouds. I then relate to this image to find out if it will be said, played on or done. I usually forget about the picture until a strong urge about it makes me aware that I can prove my visions correct. I sometimes tell people, but it ruins my ability for visions to come as naturally. I don't expect you to understand fully what I've just said, but it's not an easy thing to put into words. Picking up people's thoughts takes a longer description than the room left on the paper, so I will tell you later. Thank you for taking time to try to put this into something easier to accept.

THE CAPTIVATING FIRE

As I was coming home that afternoon I had a strange feeling that something very dramatic was going to happen to me. I didn't know who he was, but I knew he would come. I had been home for a matter of hours before I knew how I was going to meet the creator of my eerie feelings. That night I must build a fire in the determinedly unused fireplace. The fire would have to be concealed from the members of the household, so it couldn't be brought to life until everybody was unconscious and the house was still.

When the fire was at its peak, I lay down and faced it. It was indescribably beautiful. The glowing flames were tongues licking the air and snapping back. Ah! with such grace and beauty! The flames died down slowly and had almost disappeared. I watched the man form gradually, and I was calm. There appeared a bright orange figure in one of the red-hot pieces of a burnt log. The features began to show one by one. As the face became more distinct, so did my feelings toward him. I knew that I had found somebody who could understand me. He looked at me in such a way that I felt he knew everything about me.

Then suddenly, he died! The log on which he appeared burned through, splitting his face and scattering the remains. I found myself breathing hard and my heart pounding. I stared at the bits and pieces that used to make up such a knowing vision, until they, too, finally stopped glowing and lay lifeless, cold and black.

Facing Our Own Deaths

12

Let Us Live While We Are Here

Nowhere is the philosophy behind the sharing of experiences, feelings, and knowledge about death and dying more beautifully and appropriately stated than in Elisabeth Kübler-Ross' book *Death: The Final Stage of Growth.* "It is the denial of death that is partially responsible for people living empty, purposeless lives; for when you live as if you'll live forever, it becomes too easy to postpone the things you know you must do. . . . In contrast, when you fully understand that each day could be the last you have, you take the time *that day* to grow, to become more of who you really are, to reach out to other human beings. We are living in a time of uncertainty, anxiety, fear and despair. It is essential that you become aware of the light, power, and strength within each of you, and that you learn to use those inner resources in service of your own and others' growth."

Nine weeks is a short time to work with kids on changing attitudes and freeing emotions that have been long overlooked. But it was a marvelous process that we went through together. I began with the premise of fully accepting and respecting the feelings and experiences of the kids — and this bounced back to persuade me to accept my own. Before teaching those classes, I already understood intellectually this psychological principle: people should not be prevented from experiencing death fully, with a conditioned response substituted for spontaneous individual feelings. Unless we *experience* the events in our lives fully and directly, we become blocked, less able to feel, out of touch with ourselves. By the time I had taught about death and dying for three years, I knew this principle on another level altogether — understood how it actually worked in the lives of young people and in my own life.

The first result of the class studies was a greater awareness of the existence of death in the midst of life.

I have been trying to be observant about death, and what people's actions and thoughts are. When my aunt and grandmother came to visit, they gave my mother a list of where things were in their house. My mother said, "You shouldn't be worrying about things like this. Nothing is going to happen to you." This says to me that even as adults, although we know what has to happen, we still cannot accept that our parents will die, and we will be left here to live without them.

I have been watching my eight-year-old brother play with his Christmas toy, a tank that runs on remote control. It shoots out little suction cups. He came over and shot one at me shouting, "Sissy, I'm shooting you dead!" On Saturday mornings he watches cartoons. He sees characters get blown up, and then stand up again, as if nothing had happened. I think most children think that death is just not real, it is some kind of a game.

IF I DIE & WHEN I DO

"Bloody Trail Leads to Body," found on page thirteen
Chutist Surprised He Lived To Tell,
I guess he thinks it's pretty swell,
"Three Convicted in Bomb Plot, there's bombing everywhere,
A city park, a building, or perhaps a county fair.
"Blast in Mexico, hurting forty-eight,
What a shame it was, right outside the city gate.
Death is in the papers, death is in the air,
But if you stop to really think, death is everywhere.

As part of their studies, students conducted interviews to find out about community attitudes toward death, old age, and rituals connected with dying. They talked with older people, fellow students, younger kids, people whose work brought them into close contact with death. Sometimes they interviewed their own parents and shared, perhaps for the first time, ideas about the end of this life and what may come after. Here a student asks her mother questions she has prepared herself.

Me: *How do you feel about death?*
Mom: *Death is a great sadness for the people who knew the deceased. But for the deceased, if they have led a full and interesting life, death should not be feared. If they*

have been ill, death may be a relief. Death is a natural part of the life cycle.

Me: Do you believe in reincarnation?

Mom: No. I consider that one's life is complete within one life cycle.

Me: What were your feelings about the first death you experienced in your family?

Mom: That was grandfather, who I barely knew. I felt guilty that I didn't feel more sadness. Now that I look back, I realize a 10-year-old would have difficulty feeling great emotion for a relatively unknown person.

Me: Are you afraid to die?

Mom: No. If I were to die young, I would be sorry to miss my children growing up, and I would be sad not to have more years with my husband. But the thought of dying does not frighten me.

Me: How old is old?

Mom: 80! (That's because my dad is a young 74 years.)

Me: Are you afraid of aging?

Mom: No, but I do desire to do it gracefully. I have a fear of long, incurable illness.

Me: Is death the end?

Mom: When death takes place, the body dies and can never physically live again. But I believe in something my grandmother said to me: "When you die, your bones or ashes are buried in the ground. After a while they become part of the earth and you will be capable of growing a flower." That was a thrilling idea to me and I have felt no fear of death from that moment.

The person I interviewed about death was a mortician and a coroner. He said he thought children should learn about death so they will not be afraid of it. He said most people had the wrong idea about morticians, that they are old and mean and want to take your money away. He does not think death is bad.

CAN WE AlWAYS
ClOSE OUR EYES TO
DEATH?

NO!

Are you going to be one of them?

Facing Our Own Deaths

HOW SHOULD PARENTS TELL CHILDREN ABOUT DEATH?

Some parents try to hide death from their children, thinking they are doing them good. But really it isn't any good because the children will be afraid of death instead of understanding it. I think a death class should be offered in communities for parents on how to tell their children. And I think this class should be in school more often. I told my Mom about this class and she agrees, because she thinks people should learn how to help other people when they are going through the stages of death.

The following story by a student reveals an understanding of the kind of loving parental support that is needed by children facing death for the first time:

THE ACCIDENT

Eleven-year-old Ruth Haney had gotten out of the wrong side of the bed. Nothing had gone right, and it didn't seem like anything would.

She had woken up to a heavy rain, which meant a struggle with raincoat and boots, and the long, miserable walk to school. She got dressed, then crossed the hall to her 7-year-old brother's room. She knocked so hard on the door that she hurt her hand. After a few minutes, full of the sound of drawers being opened and shut, Jed stumbled out, still looking half asleep.

"Did you have a good dream or a bad dream last night?" Ruth asked.

"I had two dreams. One that Dad didn't go to Europe and the other that I got hit by a car and died."

"I doubt that will happen," Ruth said comfortingly.

Downstairs not even the cheery singing of her parakeet, Bo, nor the bright red and white checked curtains and tablecloth helped to cheer her up.

At the table, Mrs. Haney served waffles, not one of Ruth's favorite breakfasts. Before she was finished, her mother told her it was time to get ready for school. After putting on raincoats and boots, Ruth and Jed set out. Mrs. Haney called after them, "Be careful when you cross the roads. They're slippery."

"Why did it have to rain?" Ruth demanded angrily of Jed.

"I don't know, Ruth. Maybe God is crying."

They were silent the rest of the way.

School was only two blocks away now. Just as they were about to cross the street, Jed, instead of taking Ruth's hand, darted out on his own. Too late to shout a warning, Ruth saw the car, going too fast to ever stop. She shut her eyes, then heard a screech of brakes, a scream, a crash and then silence.

She opened her eyes and saw the car, a '61 Chevy, up on the sidewalk, and a small figure lying in the street. Ruth ran to her brother, screaming and crying. There was no response. She turned to run for help, but a strong pair of hands stopped her.

"I've called an ambulance. Now you must calm down."

The piercing shriek of an ambulance shattered the air, and the little crowd of school children and adults that had gathered stopped talking.

Facing Our Own Deaths

Two men wearing white uniforms carefully and slowly placed Jed on a stretcher. One man reached down and felt Jed's pulse, then covered him over with a blanket. Every inch of him.

"No! No! Not my brother!" screamed Ruth.

To herself she thought, "This can't be really happening. It's a dream. I'll wake up and everything will be fine." The last thing she remembered was the wail of the ambulance as it drove off with Jed. Then she felt her mother's arms, warm and comforting.

The next few weeks were chaos. Her mother spent ninety percent of her time with Ruth. The rest went in filling out forms, arranging the funeral, and in court. She was suing the driver of the car for speeding. If it hadn't gone so fast, Jed might have lived.

Ruth went to school, slept and ate. She spoke little, and when she did it was never about Jed.

One night Mrs. Haney decided to talk to Ruth about the accident, to help her get it all out in the open. Ruth came down the stairs, her dark hair looking almost black because of the whiteness of her face. Her mother motioned her to sit down.

"Ruth, I know it's been hard for you, first your father going off to Europe and now this. I know how you feel, because I loved Jed so much too, but just because he is gone doesn't mean that you should give up your life. Right now he's all you are thinking about, and it's probably extra hard on you because you saw it happen. But, honey, you've gotta keep going. If you don't, you'll just waste your life on someone who isn't even here. I don't want you to forget him, but guard your good memories of *him and think of them, rather than how he left us. I think it will help you feel better."*

Ruth felt hot tears coming down her face, tears that had wanted to get out much sooner. She looked at her mother's face, which was also wet with tears, and said, "I'll try, Mom. I'll really try."

A month later, Ruth was herself again, a now happy girl who had had to learn to accept death — the hard way.

Two questions that stimulated students to face their own deaths were "How would you want to die, if you had your choice?" and "What would you like to happen when you die?"

I want to die of old, old, old age! I would like to fall asleep and never wake up. Some people might want to have a quick death, like being shot or stabbed. I would rather not know that I had died. I want to die in my own house, too. I would feel more peaceful and restful.

I want to die doing something like skiing or some other sport. I don't want to die of old age, because I hate to suffer.

When death comes to me, I hope it comes when I am dreaming, in a warm bed, softly transforming me to myself.

Facing Our Own Deaths

Death is a sunset
Alone on a hill,
Tall aspen, mimicking the
Sky's gold-rimmed pastels.

A mountain slope, taking my eyes away
To the files of my mind,
Taking reality, adding, subtracting,
Stretching my life before and after.

I would like to freeze because you just get numb all over
and you can't feel it. I would want my family with me, and
my dog, and I would like to die on a mountain.

The way I wouldn't like to die is from a disease. That way
you die slowly and in pain at the end. This would be a
torture to the people who love me, I think, to see me
dying slowly and in pain. But for one reason I wouldn't
mind dying like this, because the people I love would
have time to learn to accept the fact that I was dying.

I would want some drug to kill the pain if I died slow. I
would not want to be kept alive by machines.

MY FUNERAL

My funeral will not be at a cemetery or a church. It will be
in Jackson Hole, Wyoming, up in the mountains by the
Grosse Venture River at my favorite camping spot, next

to a cottonwood tree. I'm going to be cremated and have my ashes thrown in the river. And I would like them to remember me as a venturing guy.

FLOAT ON THE WIND

*I don't know if others agree
But I disapprove of burial, you see.
The thought of me rotting
While locked in a box,
Beneath all the soil,
The dirt, and the rocks
Is depressing to me.
I'd rather be cremated
And float on the wind.*

MY DEATH

*I'm not exactly
afraid of death,
it's beyond death
that really bothers me.
On my death
I hope people don't cry,
and don't sigh,
but sing that I was once alive,
and that I brought
a new life into the world.*

AFTER MY DEATH

After my death I would like to have my family decide if they wanted me to have a funeral. I don't really care how I die, but I would prefer to die in my sleep. When I die, I want my stuff to go to my family, except for my trophies. I would want my friend John to have them. I am going to give my body to science.

FOR MY HEADSTONE

I just want to say
I wish I could
Have loved more
And hated less.

I like the thought of my ashes blowing in the wind, or in the ocean, or in the mountains. Somewhere beautiful. I can understand people not liking the thought of being burned, but you are dead anyway. When you're buried, all you're doing is wasting land.

Another challenge was to try to face the question, "What would you do if you had only a short time left to live?"

IF I WERE DYING OF CANCER

I would probably go out of my mind. But my parents would keep me calm. I would want to do my favorite sports, and fly to Germany to see all my relatives. I would look how everyone looks and acts, and probably I would learn to appreciate everything a little bit more. In the end, I would come to accept the fact that I was dying.

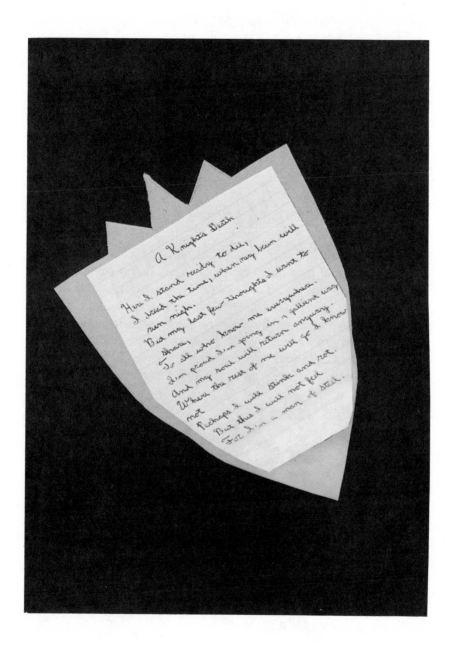

A Knight's Death

Here I stand ready to die,
I dread the time, when my doom will
run nigh.
But my last few thoughts I want to
share,
To all who know me everywhere.
I'm proud I'm going in a gallent way,
And my soul will return anyway.
Where the rest of me will go I know
not.
Perhaps I will stink and rot.
But this I will not feel.
For I'm a man of steel.

IF I HAD ONE MONTH TO LIVE

First of all, I wouldn't believe whoever told me. I just am positive I wouldn't. I'd feel angry at any person who told me this. Then, I think I would begin to appreciate everything I took for granted, at least a little bit. I probably would have a lot more love for my family than I do now. After that, I'm sure I'd begin to feel sorry for myself and kinda pouty. But knowing that I didn't have long to live, I'd eventually "snap out" of it.

IF I HAD TO DIE EARLY

I would try not to think about my dying early. I'd make every day count. I would do all the things I would have done later on in my life. I would move up to our cabin in the mountains and live up there forever. I would climb every mountain in sight. I'd live every day I had left with a smile. When The Day came, I would remember my happy life. I am not really afraid to die.

IF I KNEW I WAS GOING TO DIE

What most people want to do when they know they're going to die is take a trip around the world. I don't think I could do that. I would just hope that those last days could be the happiest memories in my whole life. I would try to help others more than myself, because I think that would make me the happiest. I don't have any special wishes for my funeral, but I just hope all of my family and friends would come 'cause I think it's like me giving them a goodbye for a while.

FACING MY OWN DEATH

Franki, once a doctor told me I was dying, and I believed him, so I was dying. Then, I thought, I haven't seen enough to be dying yet. So I started fighting. It was a long fight, and I thought I had lost it a few times, but I wasn't about to give up. I learned a lot from this experience, and I hope I can share it with you. I hope you can always be totally aware of what's going on, because there is so much to experience and I wouldn't want you to miss anything. With love.

As the course continued, an increasing number of students expressed their understanding of the need to accept death. They began to see it as a part of life, as inevitable and inescapable.

NO ESCAPE

He ran swiftly
through the field,
the grass tickled
his bare legs.

The night was cool,
the sky was painted
pink, orange and yellow.

He kept running,
trying to escape
a problem, death!

He tried to run
faster,
but staggered.

He faltered,
then stumbled
and fell.

Then he realized
everyone
has to face death.

DEATH MUST COME

It may come when
we are not expecting
it to, or wanting it to,
but it will come.
We must learn to accept
death, for if and when
we do, if someone dies
it may be easier,
knowing everyone will die.

SHARING

The difference between you and me
may be our way of living,
the way we love, the way we care
and what it is we're giving.
But there is something that we share,
while we live our lives a lie,
and that's the way that we should both
accept it, when we die.

THINKING

I think if I had one
Wish I might wish never
To die but to see all
The generations go by but
I don't have a wish so I
Guess me and everyone else
Will have to learn to accept
Death. It will be hard and
May take a long time but
When we do it very well
May be mans greatest
Accomplishment.

death
  does
not
  come
  sweetly
nor
  does
  it
come
   gracefully
but
  it
  is
there
  waiting
  to
   take
you
  into
  its
  rough
  arms
waiting
  to
  bring
  sadness
  to
your
  loved
   ones
it
  is
there
don't
  hide

for
  death
loves
  to
    take
those
  that
are
  fearful
live
  for
  now
    don't
just
  run
  from
death
  for life
is worth more
  than
death
  life
is
  stronger
& handsome
to
  those who
behold it.

WHAT WILL I GAIN?

I often think I am stuck with life
I'm riddled with misery, discomfort and strife.
People say to keep hanging on, 'cause one day
Good luck and fortune will come my way.

But it's not good luck and fortune I seek,
It's wisdom and knowledge that I must reach.
Why should I speak out or struggle in vain
If there's no one to listen, what will I gain?

I may not gain wisdom, attention or wealth
But I'll have peace and contentment within myself.
Yes, it's worth the suffering, torment, pain
To reach the wisdom I wish to obtain.

I will live my life to the fullest each day
And when my time comes to slip away,
I'll be so happy, oh, please don't weep,
I've just fallen into an infinite sleep.

This student's talk of torment and struggle were not mere sentimental words. At the time she wrote this, she was facing an abusive home situation and the possibility of dying of leukemia.

Another student wrote:

Not even a year ago, a person very close to me died.
I blamed God — I thought He didn't love my friend.
But now I am coming to understand that everyone
dies, even someone you love as much as you possibly
can.

WHY AM I AFRAID TO DIE?

I wonder if I'm in God's eye?
If I'm not, maybe that's why
I'm afraid to die.
If death came today,

Would I not be afraid?
I know it's around the bend,
Will I be scared then?
It has to come sometime.
When it does, I hope I'm not terrified
Because when it's here, you can't turn back.
When it appears, I'll try not to fear
I must accept it, fear or not,
Because it's a fact.

The most characteristic, human, and exhilarating response to admitting the role of death in their existence brought the students an enhanced sense of life and a heightened awareness of the importance of finding their unique identity.

A SEED REALIZING

A seed beginning its first root
Not knowing what it is
But hoping for the best
Growing inch by inch
Day by day
The world outside goes on
Not knowing when it will come up
The soil so soft
Moving for anything
Its first peek above the ground
Finding everything
Realizing it is
A flower.

(The student brought me a small plant with this poem.)

THE COLOR OF EMOTIONS

Sometimes I cry when I feel like laughing,
pretend I'm dying when I'm really happy.
I am responsible for my actions, when I laugh,
cry, smile, and even when I just sit, wondering.
Emotion — what is it, where is it, why is it?
How is it that I change? Do people make me,
or as I grow older, bigger, do I lose
contact with the real "me," myself?

To you perhaps colors are just colors,
to me they have meanings: purple-orchid
is mellow but quick to be irritated,
orange-red is exasperation, yellow is happy,
green is my favorite color, outdoorsy,
it makes me feel trapped and it encourages me to get
untrapped, to reach my goal. It makes me
ambitious. I like that.

WHO AM I?

"Be yourself!" "Don't put on an act!" That seems to be
what everyone tells me. Be yourself — but what is my-
self? I act about twenty different ways. I can't help it.
Different situations call for different ways to act. I have
hundreds of different personalities. Is "being yourself"
being quiet and very sophisticated? That's what it seems
like: whenever I'm told to be myself, I'm either being very
loud or trying to "impress" somebody by supposedly
acting better than I am. Nobody ever tells me to be myself
when I'm quiet and acting very mature. What makes
adults, like Mom and Dad, think they know exactly what
"myself" is? They don't know who I am, any more than I
know who they are.

THE LOST YEARS

*The girl walked through the field, not noticing anything.
She didn't smell the wonderful scents.*

*She came again the next year. She noticed the beauty,
but couldn't appreciate the scent.*

*When she had been married twenty years, she came
back. She noticed the beauty and the peacefulness, but
she still didn't smell the scent.*

*She came back when she was near death. She observed
the beauty, the peacefulness — and the scent. She wept
for all those years when she didn't notice the perfume of
the flowers.*

WHAT COULD HAVE BEEN

*I run swiftly, silently,
into the dark tunnel of death.*

*I close my eyes,
thinking of what could have been.*

*The children who are not to be,
flowers that I didn't see,
holding on to what I've got,
feeling bad about when we fought,
nothing really happening,
just visions of
what could have been.*

BEING ALIVE

I will be buried in the mountains.
I will grow old in the mountains.
When I die I won't be worried.

I know the sky will be crisp blue,
The storms will rage with anger
But the anger will end.
The winter snows will melt,
The spring flowers will bloom.

On the outside I'm afraid,
But on the inside I know
The world will still live on.

I am curious to know
What lies ahead, beyond death,
But I know, and always will,
There is no place as peaceful
And as beautiful as being alive
Here, now, forever.

WHERE DID IT GO?

Where did it go, so fast, so quick?
As I look back on life,
It started only yesterday.

Where did it go? What did I do?
Could I have made better
Use of the days?

Did I care enough?
Did I share enough?
Where did it go?

As my day ends on earth
I will be given a new birth.
I gave it the best I could.
Where did it go?

NOTHING FOREVER

A minute ago this paper was blank,
Now words fill the page,
But one day this paper and these words
Will rot away forever.

At first this land was flat,
Now it is a mountain
And some day man will level it
To build houses.

At first I was not even here,
Now I am alive
And one day I too
Will cease to exist.

Not words, not a mountain
Nor even a life
Will exist forever.

But one thing I'm sure of is that the words
on the paper can be good words, and the
mountain can be a home for many living
creatures, and my life can be a life
that brings happiness to others.

I'd like the memory of me
To be a happy one.
I'd like to leave an afterglow
Of smiles when life is done.
I'd like to leave an echo
Whispering softly down the ways,
Of happy times, and laughing times
and bright and sunny days.
I'd like the tears of those who grieve
To dry before the sun.

Of happy memories I leave
Behind – when life is done.

A LITTLE PRAYER

Life so sweet,
Life so dear,
Let us live
While we are here!
Amen.

A TENDER THING, LIFE

Death,
I fear it,
My friends' sorrows,
the unknown possibilities.
I fear life after death
for, like death, it is an unexplored subject.

It is a tender thing, life,
It is here one second,
the next, gone.
But what can our opinions mean?
We are the living,
we have no knowledge,
true and factual knowledge,
about the abrupt word,
Death.

Who are we to say,
"Death is a bleak, gruesome and terrible thing.
It is haunted with mysterious black,
and dull colors."
For all we know it could really
be explained as
the unusual and rewarding experience.
The troubles and pains of life gone,
no hassles. Beautiful.

Now
Live your life without being burdened with death.
Get everything you can out of life,
but don't give a care about the small things
or big that don't work out perfectly.
For all we know
Everything works out, in the end.

Suggested Activities

13

Below is a list of activities I have used in teaching young people about death. It is hoped that these suggestions will encourage the reader to create additional activities for personal and group exploration.

1. Students share in writing, verbally and/or in art form, their first experience with death.
2. Students express in some creative way — a poem, story, picture, song, collage, play — what death means to them.
3. Students share what they believe about life after death and how they formed those beliefs.
4. Students plan, describe, and perhaps act out their own funeral.
5. Students role-play how they would tell their own child about the death of a pet, a relative, or a friend.
6. Students visit a graveyard, walk around for 15 minutes, and then write or draw their feelings. (Collect epitaphs, make grave rubbings, make hypotheses

about the community and the people from the information on the gravestones, compare old and new parts of the cemetery, etc.)

7. Students discuss the many ways people die and tell how they would choose to die.
8. Students interview their parents and grandparents concerning experiences and beliefs about aging, death, and after death.
9. Students visit a mortuary to gather information about their purposes and procedures. Share feelings and experiences.
10. Students talk with terminally ill people about their process.
11. Students share in writing, verbally and/or in art form, their most vivid nightmares and dreams about death.
12. Students keep a dream diary and become aware of what parts death plays in their dreams.
13. Students share a "small death" in their lives (e.g., separation from friends, divorce).
14. Students use relaxation exercises and guided imagery to take a journey to the time of their own deaths. Afterward, they share what happened to them verbally and/or in pictures, poems, stories. (Jeffrey Schrank, 1972)
15. Students visit a nursing home, and talk with patients, nurses, doctors, and aides about living and dying in a nursing home.
16. Students help to create a special area in the classroom to display their own and their teachers' questions. (As questions are answered, remove them; discuss the remaining Big Questions for which there are no ready-made answers.) (Dee Coulter)
17. Students talk with people in the community who have strong and varied attitudes and experiences with death (e.g., someone on the suicide prevention team, a minister who counsels the dying, a person who has been clinically "dead" and revived, an elderly man or

woman with good health and a zest for living). Suggestions: (1) Involve students in the process of locating these resource people; (2) Look for people who can relate to young people.

18. Students use relaxation exercises and guided imagery to travel in time to the age of 75. Afterward they share as much as they can of their life as a 75-year-old person (physical appearance, activities, environment, feelings, and thoughts, and what death means to them at that period in their lives).

19. Students visit a "hospice" organization in the community.

20. Students, in small groups, research and present in a creative way the death-related customs and beliefs from various cultures and religions (beliefs about what causes death, what comes after death, burial customs, mourning rituals, etc.).

21. Students seek out and share music, short stories, poems, articles, artwork, etc. that speak personally to them about death.

22. Students survey death-related television shows to investigate how the subject of death is treated by the media. Share personal reactions.

23. Students write a list of personal beliefs about death, and explore the sources of these beliefs (e.g., religion, family, school, culture).

24. Students write a Bill of Rights for all people regarding the process of dying.

25. Students debate relevant political and legal issues regarding death (e.g., euthanasia and the right to die).

Postscript

As my classes on death and dying drew to a close, two colleagues and I took twenty students on a camping trip to Rocky Mountain National Park. It was there, around the campfire, that I finally gave up the rest of my limiting beliefs about age.

We were together effortlessly, making fires, cleaning up, hiking, and talking. One evening I was sitting by the fire and drinking a cup of coffee. Some students joined me, and we began a discussion that roamed over many subjects, but focused finally on the love they felt for one another. Then one young person disclosed that she had leukemia, and although she had not wanted to share her situation, she had been doing a great deal of work on the possibility of her death. After a period of silence there was a wave of emotional sharing. Then another young woman talked of her struggle over several years with a life-threatening illness. The two exchanged their feelings and what they had learned from their relationship with illness and the possibility of death at an early age. As they talked, I saw several things they felt in common:

They had taken responsibility for their illnesses and felt that they were healing themselves.

They felt life was an extraordinary gift to be lived with zest and joy, and they believed that most people didn't realize this.

They felt that awareness of death had been a gift to bring them into a deeper appreciation of life.

One of my 14-year-old friends took my hand and said, with the campfire light dancing in her eyes, "We love you."

What had begun as a common interest in death had resulted in a deep and crisp awareness of the gifts of life, love, and friendship, and an enduring gratitude for what I had learned from all my young teachers.

Bibliography

Today there are many resources available in the area of death education. We offer a brief list of some of the written resources that were helpful in teaching about this subject.

"A Special Issue on Death and Dying: Transforming the Fears and Myths," *New Age,* November 1979.

Adler, Charles, Gene Stanford, and Sheila Morrissey Adler, eds., *We Are But a Moment's Sunlight: Understanding Death.* New York: Pocket Books, 1976.

Becker, Ernest, *The Denial of Death.* New York: Macmillan, 1973.

Bender, David L., ed., *Problems of Death.* Opposing Viewpoints Series, Vol. 8. Anoka, Minn.: Greenhaven Press, 1974.

Cook, Sarah Sheets, *Children and Dying: An Exploration and Selective Bibliographies.* New York: Health Sciences Publishing Corp., 1974.

Death: An Experimental Unit. Center for Teaching International Relations. University of Denver, Colorado.

Faraday, Ann, *The Dream Game.* New York: Harper & Row, 1974.

Garfield, Patricia, *Creative Dreaming.* New York: Ballantine Books, 1974.

Hendricks, Gay, and Russell Wills, *The Centering Book: Awareness Activities for Children, Parents and Teachers.* Englewood Cliffs, N.J.: Prentice-Hall, 1975.

Hendricks, Gay, and Thomas B. Roberts, *The Second Centering Book: More Awareness Activities for Children, Parents and Teachers.* Englewood Cliffs, N.J.: Prentice-Hall, 1977.

Hendricks, Gay, and James Fadiman, eds., *Transpersonal Education: A Curriculum for Feeling and Being.* Englewood Cliffs, N.J.: Prentice-Hall, 1976.

. . . I Never Saw Another Butterfly . . . Children's Drawings and Poems from Terezín Concentration Camp 1942—1944. New York: McGraw-Hill, 1964.

Jury, Mark and Dan, *Gramp.* New York: Viking Penguin, 1976.

Kübler-Ross, Elisabeth, *On Death and Dying.* New York: Macmillan, 1969.

Kübler-Ross, Elisabeth, *Death: The Final Stage of Growth*. Englewood Cliffs, N.J.: Prentice-Hall, 1975.

Lewis, Howard R., and Dr. H. Streitfeld, *Growth Games: How to Tune in Yourself, Your Family, Your Friends*. New York: Bantam Books, 1972.

Mannes, Marya, *Last Rights: A Case for the Good Death*. New York: New American Library, 1973.

Masters, Robert, and Jean Houston, *Mind Games: The Guide to Inner Space*. New York: Dell, 1972.

Moody, Raymond, *Life After Life*. Harrisburg, Pa.: Stackpole, 1973.

Morgan, Ernest et al., eds., *A Manual of Death Education and Simple Burial*. Burnsville, N.C.: The Celo Press, 1975.

Popenoe, Chris, *The Yes! Guide: Books for Inner Development*. Washington D.C.: Yes! Bookshop, 1976.

Samuels, Mike, and Nancy Samuels, *Seeing With the Mind's Eye: The History, Techniques and Uses of Visualization*. New York: Random House, 1975.

Schrank, Jeffrey, *Teaching Human Beings: 101 Subversive Activities for the Classroom*. Boston: Beacon Press, 1972.

Staffard, David D., "Should the Study of Death be a Necessary Preparation for Living?", *Controversial Issues in the Social Studies: A Contemporary Perspective*. In *45th Yearbook of the National Council for the Social Studies*. (1201 16th St., N.W. Washington, D.C., 1975.)